6.95

JOY TO THE WORLD:

An Introduction to Kingdom Evangelism

ROBERT T. HENDERSON

John Knox Press
ATLANTA

Library of Congress Cataloging in Publication Data

Henderson, Robert T   1928–
  Joy to the world.

  Includes bibliographical references.
  1. Evangelistic work.   2. Kingdom of God.
I. Title.
BV3790.H387   269'.2   80–14597
ISBN 0–8042–2096–4

Printed in the United States of America
John Knox Press
Atlanta, Georgia 30308

CONTENTS

DEDICATION

Dedicated to Virgil and Mildred, my parents, who birthed me, prayed for me, evangelized me, modeled the Christian life for me, and have surrounded me with love all of my life.

INTRODUCTION

For the past three years I have been passing myself off as the denominational wizard in evangelism. Now, when you're a member of an "establishment" denomination in the United States, that does not mean you are operating in any hotbed of evangelistic superstars. But it does mean that you spend a lot of time with a lot of people, who, to the best of their knowledge, really intend to be faithful to Jesus Christ and to his church.

It also means, however, that you are forever dealing with caricatures, confusion, and consternation over the whole discipline of evangelism. For whatever reasons, most of the people that I have been dealing with know that Jesus Christ is good news but at the same time just are not comfortable with most of the packaged plans or programs which are supposed to produce "effective evangelism." So let me confess: I'm not comfortable with them either! I know that such a confession may sound heretical coming out of a teacher of evangelism. So be it. I might be charged with being cowardly or unspiritual. Both may be true.

Let me go on with my confession. Basically, I'm a shy person, and I have some sensitive feelings. I will never be a good salesperson. When I was a kid I would try selling flower seeds from door to door. I used the classic low-pressure, almost-sure-to-fail sales technique: "You don't want to buy any seeds, do you?"

I didn't want to offend anyone else, and I didn't want to be rejected. I also didn't like anyone else putting pressure on me. I have the same reservations about packaged sales techniques in evangelism. I've seldom seen evangelism that really satisfied me which came as a packaged program. Maybe that's my own hang-up. But, if so, I have a lot of company.

Granted, there are a whole lot of gifted and aggressive

9

Christians who go out with evangelistic sales techniques and do, in fact, bring blessing to others. I know many of them and thank God for them. I have even engaged in some planned market-place "blitzes" myself and know for a fact that this has its place. Having said all of that, I still don't believe that such is the normative New Testament pattern.

Another area that has always left me dissatisfied is the content of most evangelistic programs with which I am familiar. I remember reading one renowned ecumenical theologian who said that the whole Christian message could be summarized under "guilt and forgiveness." Listen, when a big name theologian says something like that you're supposed to be impressed! But the university folks with whom I was dealing at the time didn't feel guilty about anything. The issue they were grappling with was the question of the meaning of life. I knew that Jesus spoke to the issue of meaning; yet, there were some pieces not in place in my own mind. What was the basic theme of Jesus' ministry?

Added to all those kinds of unresolved questions in my mind was the obvious biblical fact that my evangelistic heritage made a lot more of a priority of evangelism than did the apostles. Evangelism is almost never mentioned in the epistles. It is even difficult to describe the charismatic gift of "evangelist," which is mentioned only twice, I think, in the New Testament. Those early Christians were obviously very conscious of the world and of the society of non-Christian persons out there. Yet the apostles write to them almost exclusively about ordering the internal affairs of their congregational life. Why is this?

This book, then, is something of a record of my own biblical and practical pilgrimage in the area of evangelism. I invite you to join me. I have become really charged up with what I have discovered. If I am a bit irreverent with some of the hoary traditions of evangelicalism, I trust you can smile, and forgive me!

About the style and motif, let me say a word. First, about style. A few years ago, Betty (my wife) and I were at a weekend conference and were looking over the book table. I was aghast at what seemed to me to be ditty-bop, pop-Christian trivia, which they were selling. I voiced my feelings to Betty. Her response was that most theologically articulate persons write books for other theologically articulate persons, so that laypersons have to resort to the short, popular Christian peperbacks which they can understand. Then she challenged me, if I were ever to write a book that I would do it in such a popular fashion that it could be read, digested, and put into practice by the ordinary, garden-variety, thoughtful layperson. For this reason the content of *Joy to the World* is purposely introductory and popular. But it is subtitled "An *Introduction* to Kingdom Evangelism," indicating that there is a whole wealth of heavy theological content beyond what is presented here.

The designation "kingdom evangelism" deserves a word. It is the clue to the motif. I was asked why I did not just call it "Christian evangelism." The wording is deliberate. One of the most thrilling and inescapable facts in New Testament study is that Jesus, in the three Synoptic Gospels (Matthew, Mark, and Luke), almost universally speaks of the gospel as the "gospel of the kingdom."

> "And this gospel of the kingdom will be preached throughout the whole world, as a testimony to all nations; and then the end will come."
>
> (Matt. 24:14)

That is our clue. That designation, "the gospel of the kingdom," is the overarching description of the joyous news (gospel) which came to us in Jesus of Nazareth.

I want to pursue that theme within the framework of three disciplines (or what have been classically termed "Christian formations"):

A. Understanding the Joyous News of the Kingdom of God
B. Experiencing the Joyous News of the Kingdom of God
C. Obeying the Joyous News of the Kingdom of God

Please be aware that I will use *joyous news, gospel,* and *evangel* interchangeably, since they all come from the Greek word *euangelion,* meaning "joyous news or announcement."

I have taught this material to scores of workshops, classes, and congregations. I have become increasingly excited that in this theme are pieces that complete the picture of the evangelistic task. May God be pleased to use this study to liberate a great host to be the joyous and spontaneous instruments of kingdom evangelism.

> "JOY TO THE WORLD! THE LORD IS COME:
> LET EARTH RECEIVE HER KING."
> (Isaac Watts, 1719)

SECTION I
Understanding the Joyous News of the Kingdom of God

"I send you to open their eyes, that they may turn from darkness to light and from the power of Satan to God, that they may receive forgiveness of sins and a place among those who are sanctified by faith in me."

(The ascended Jesus to Saul of Tarsus
Acts 26:17–18)

CHAPTER 1
What's the Problem?

I always get a little amused at the kind of person whose response to almost any personal question is: "Why? What's wrong?" But having said that, I must add that this is a most natural question as one begins to explore the discipline of evangelism. The very word "gospel" means "joyous news" and has all kinds of overtones of fulfilled expectation, of joyous hope, and of experienced liberation. Yet those tones all imply that something has been awry that is now being made right. And it doesn't really make a lot of sense to talk of answers until you know what the problem is. So, what's the problem?

There are all kinds of places you can look for descriptions of the problem: the daily news, literature, philosophy, or history. Even poetry and the top ten popular songs are excellent voices. But for starts let's look at some biblical teachings. The good news of Jesus Christ the Son of God didn't come into a vacuum. "The light shines in the darkness," states the evangelist John. Darkness! At the very least that implies some kind of evil environment.

Later, when Peter is telling the awestruck crowd at Jerusalem what all the pentecostal noise is about, he challenges them to save themselves from "this crooked age." But when the ascended Jesus calls Saul of Tarsus into his service, his charge to Saul is: "I send you to open their eyes (they are blind), and to turn them from darkness to light (they are in the dark), from the dominion of Satan to God (they are captive to an alien power). . . ." That's enough to start with. It is enough to dispel any notion that people are neutral and free in and of themselves.

The New Testament speaks throughout of the clash between powers or dominions. The alien power is the dominion of darkness (Col. 1:13), the dominion of death (Rom. 6:9), the dominion of sin (Rom. 6:14), or the dominion of Satan (Acts 26:18). The thrust is clear. The dominion of Satan is destructive and tragic even though it forever disguises itself as seeking the welfare of its subjects. The clash of powers comes out in almost epic form in The Revelation to John where the warfare between the beast and the Lamb is portrayed. The dominion of Satan is far more than a personal problem. It is corporate and systemic, as in "save yourselves from this crooked (screwed-up) generation" (Acts 2:40).

The darkness may be moral, intellectual, or cultural. It is dark because there is no light to show the way. It appears also that one may be in the power or dominion of darkness (or Satan) by choice, or as a victim of a system where one is helpless. That is to say that some are hell-raisers by choice: they love the darkness; they couldn't care less about right or wrong, truth or error. Others are longing for right, for truth, but there seems to be only darkness. Some are poor, oppressed, hungry, and homeless in cultures and societies of darkness where nobody cares, where despair descends like a dark night.

How Did We Get into This Mess?

How did we get into this mess? Especially, how did we get into it when God created all things and "saw everything that he had made, and behold it was very good" (Gen. 1:31)? How do we get darkness and Satan into that?

Heavy question! Can you accept the presence of mystery? That God in his great freedom could create this world with the freedom to live in or reject his gracious domain? His creatures were not programmed to obey him. Can you accept the fact that God knew the potential of his own creation for devotion or rebellion?

And Satan? That's a bigger mystery still! There he is:

created yet supernatural, and destructively malicious. Oddly enough, the Bible never bothers to deal with his origins. A serpent in Genesis, and that old serpent the devil in Revelation. An accuser in Job, and the great tempter of Jesus in the Gospels. Some have tried to explain him away as a myth, but the explanation somehow seems unconvincing. There he is, in all his malignant display: a liar and the father of lies, a murderer, and the god of this world who blinds the eyes of those who believe not lest the light of the glorious gospel of Christ should shine in them and they should be saved (John 8:44; 2 Cor. 4:4). The reality of this evil personality, difficult as it may be to comprehend, is a teaching of scripture. We need to come to grips with its results both in the systems of this world, and in individual persons.

In the simplest biblical terms here is what happened:

Point One: God made everything that is, and it was very good. God expressed his character and will creatively. This is his glory, the expression of himself in the act of creation. The creation was harmonious and in harmony with himself; it was "holy." The Creator and the creation were together in the *shalom* (peace) of God.

Point Two: The serpent challenged the character of God and the purpose of God. In essence the serpent accused God of being something of a petty bully with no right to tell Adam and Eve what they could do. He insinuated that God and humankind were the same kind of being. To that he added the suggestion that God's purpose in instructing Adam and Eve was demeaning and dehumanizing. The challenge went on to say that if Adam and Eve should assert their autonomy and eat of the fruit (or experience the knowledge of good and evil) they would be like God. What happened then was the tragic violation of the character and purpose of God, that is, the violation of God's glory. In their God-given freedom Adam and Eve chose to rebel against their Creator. In their attempt to be like God they lost touch with the meaning of their humanity. And the reverberations were

cosmic: "The whole creation groans. . . ." Adam and Eve
had unwittingly chosen an alien authority. Darkness de-
scended upon creation. In broader biblical understanding one could say at this point God's heart was broken.
God wept even while he was angry. He was angry because he loves so infinitely.

Point Three: The result is the dominion of darkness.
Human beings are estranged from the God who made
them for himself. Cut off from the source of life, they
become lonely. Values are rearranged and distorted. In
futile attempts to fill the void they make their own gods
by deifying such mysterious dimensions of creation as
fertility, knowledge, nature, and the celestial bodies. And
lurking in the shadows is the Prince of Darkness, Satan.
The darkness permeates society, economics, govern-
ments, religion, and nature. What you have is a rebellion
that produces an alien authority that does not acknowledge the character and purpose of the God to whom all
things belong. The kingdom of darkness is established.
To be sure, the evidences of the dominion of darkness
continue among us. Our own rebellion manifests itself
today in the autonomous spirit that resents the claims of
God upon us, and that also produces alienation between
individuals, not to mention social, ethnic, and national
groupings. (I really do not want to get into the discussion
as to whether these biblical references from Genesis are
symbolic/mythical, or literal/historical. The problem of
evil is one of the profound questions of human existence,
and fraught with mystery. At least these teachings point
us in the direction of an answer. They are charged with
spiritual insights, and the whole of the rest of scripture
points back to these primitive accounts. Let us accept
their validity and move on.)

Let me begin to develop a scenario for you. It will reflect the
three points above. The first act opens, and in scene one we
thrill to the act of creation. Light and joy and freshness declare

the Creator's skill and glory. His words, "Very good," resound over everything he has made. The orchestra plays the overture to creation, reflecting the ecstasy and harmony of it all.

But in the next scene a discordant and malicious figure intrudes, and innocence is destroyed. The creation no longer declares joy in its Creator but, rather, independence from him. His gracious character and will are violated. The scene becomes dark as the whole creation groans at the tragedy of such rebellion. Now the orchestration becomes dissonant and ominous. As the dominion of darkness is established, Satan would seem to have triumphed. Except—just before the curtain drops on act one, the Creator speaks a simple word of hope, as though he had known all along of this tragic turn of events. He says: "The seed of a woman shall bruise the serpent's head. . . ." As he thus speaks, ever so subtly and pianissimo, a new and harmonious theme of joy feeds into the otherwise heavy and ominous and dissonant orchestration. The curtain falls.

For now, I want you to dwell on this tragedy of sin, this imaginary portrait of the domain of darkness which I have tried to help you visualize. I want you to recognize how sad, how utterly tragic is this human scene apart from the infinitely holy, loving, and true God. Secular humanists of our day have tried to evangelize us with the idea of human fulfillment without reference to God—but that doesn't get at the root of the problem. Let's look at the domain of darkness through the eyes of scripture and human experience and see what it is like.

There is in the Bible a whole category of words that describe the lifestyle and mind-set of persons in the dominion of darkness. These are words such as *sin, evil, evildoers, wicked,* and the *flesh.* There are nuances and hues that distinguish each of these, but the basic idea is that human beings leave God, by whom and for whom all things exist, out of their living and their thinking. They may do this passively or out of ignorance on the one hand. Or they may destructively and maliciously resent God and their neighbor on the other. But God is not at all in their thoughts. They live life on a merely natural plane. Sin can be an *act* that departs from righteousness and the righteous

God. It can also be a *quality* opposed to truth and the God of truth. Sin is often described in almost personal terms as a ruling power, a power which deceives, blinds, enslaves, and leads to destruction.

One of those catch-all words that describes the ethos of the dominion of darkness is the word *evil.* It has to do with individual and corporate humanity out of harmony with the character and purpose of God. Paul speaks of "the present evil age" (Gal. 1:4). Jesus teaches us to pray: "Deliver us from [the] evil" (Matt. 6:13). I've been pondering the different facets of "evil" that appear in the Bible, or the different faces of sin. Here are at least a few of them.

Personal Evil

The ethos of the dominion of darkness has tragic effects on the persons God created to walk in joyous and fulfilling relationship with himself. The Bible comes up with descriptions, so easily demonstrable from the daily newspaper, such as: lost, ignorant, enslaved, dead, without hope, guilty, blind, and forever flipping out over false ideologies and manufactured gods. In one brief passage a biblical writer describes us, apart from Christ, as "helpless," "ungodly," "sinners" and "enemies" (Rom. 5:6–11). These are biblical descriptions of the dilemma.

But look around you. All of this is corroborated in the weekly newsmagazine. Look at our increasing dependence on counselors and psychiatrists, and the psycho-babble that betrays our confused lives. Or look at the whole consumer mentality that brainwashes us with the notion that the possession of things will provide us with happiness, true friends, greater life meaning, and kissing-fresh breath.

False gods are everywhere present. We look to the national government as god to provide us security and economic welfare. We look to the economy as god to give us our daily bread, and when the Dow-Jones average drops ten points we panic. Or we make a god of physical, sexual, athletic pleasure, worshiping before the altars of youth, health, and vigor.

Occasionally, through all of our attempts to live without God, some perceptive playwright or author will remind us that life is absurd, as indeed it is, apart from God. Or despair creeps in to disturb our false security. The optimist says, "We live in the best of all possible worlds." And the despairing pessimist responds, "Yes, that's what I'm afraid of!" Escapism, massification (a term coined by Theodore Roszak [*Person/Planet*] to express that conspiracy of cultural and social forces that militates against unique personhood, that attempts to create the mass person without any consideration for ethnic origins, tastes, desires, or diversity of personality), drugs, entertainment, endless football games—but it's no use. We are a society without soul!

Interpersonal Evil

Contiguous to personal evil is interpersonal evil, that whole area of destructive relationships. This week on the television there have been specials on troubled families and on divorce. Right away in the Garden of Eden episode (Gen. 3), Adam blames Eve for their troubles. In the next chapter one of their sons murders the other out of jealousy. From there it is downhill. Barriers go up between persons and between tribes/nations. Family feuds abound. Romeo can't marry Juliet because he's a Montague and she's a Capulet and their families are enemies.

Paul lists strife, jealousy, anger, selfishness, and dissention as the expressions of the flesh. He regularly exhorts the church to avoid quarreling lest they behave as mere human beings rather than as the people of God. Lovelessness, indifference to human need, cruelty—these all violate the purposes and will of God.

Systemic Evil

Broader and more inclusive than interpersonal evil is what I will call "systemic evil." There are economic, political, cultural, military, educational—and even ecclesiastical—systems that oppress people and so violate the purpose of God. "Prin-

cipalities and powers . . . world rulers of this present darkness"
Paul calls them. They are the nations, the corporations, the
zeitgeists, the uncontrollable forces of the world that enslave
and darken people, and oppose the forces of righteousness.

Systemic evil is somehow more than the aggregate of evil
persons. One Christian writer defines principalities and powers
as any human institution that demands for itself devotion that
belongs only to God, be it a nation, a labor union, a corporation, a
university, or, alas, the institutional church! "Power corrupts."
"Systems, of themselves, are oppressive." Such comments are
common currency. How do you explain this? Where are the
handles on the forces, the spirits, those intangible forces that
blight, discourage, and control our lives? They are spiritual, they
are insidious, and they are beyond human control. Even those
who are united to Christ do not escape the strength and guile of
these powers. They are a mystery, and yet they are so real.

The Hapless Victims of Systemic Evil

I want deliberately to stop right here and underline a whole
theme that is a result of systemic evil, namely, the hapless victims of systemic evil. It is remarkable how much we tend to
overlook this theme in our considerations of evangelism. Here
are the helpless poor, the hungry, the homeless, the physically
blind, deaf, and diseased. Here also are those who are oppressed
by unjust economic, political, and legal powers.

These real people—millions of them—are the special objects
of divine compassion. Look at the guidelines laid down in the
Levitical code for the provision God intends his priestly nation
to make for such helpless folk. Or note the anger of Yahweh as
he speaks through the prophets about his people's failure to do
this (e.g., Isa. 58—61). Hear Jesus announcing that the Spirit of
the Lord is upon him to annoint him "to preach good news to
the poor . . . release to the captives . . . recovering of sight to
the blind" (Luke 4:18).

Of course there are people who are *spiritually* poor, blind,
lost, and fractured; but these of whom we are talking here are

victims, in a concrete and *physical* sense, of powers and systems beyond their control. When we're describing the kingdom of darkness we dare not be oblivious to these millions of helpless ones who are the victims of that kingdom. John Updike, the novelist, writes of lascivious suburbanites who go to church regularly while engaging in endless adulterous ventures with the same people they go to church with. That's in the category of *personal evil.* But Mother Teresa of Calcutta goes to the sick and helpless outcasts of Indian society who are left in the gutters to die. Her Christian compassion is toward the victims of the overwhelming *systems of evil.* Do you see the difference?

And That's Not All

There are other dimensions we could include in helping to paint the picture of the kingdom of darkness. Sometimes the light becomes darkness: religion becomes part of the problem; education may darken and confuse. Even the helping professions can be subverted and deny the Creator and his good purpose for his creation.

The gifts of nature, of beauty, air, water, soil, seedtime and harvest, given to us by God, are spoiled, misused, raped, and plundered without conscience.

This is clearly illustrated in J. R. R. Tolkien's epic *The Lord of the Rings.* The shire is inhabited by simple, industrious folk who sing, tell stories, keep neat homes and gardens, and love a good time. They love beauty, have respect for parents and traditions. But when the evil figure Saruman sends his bullies to occupy the shire the result is oppression, confusion, slavery, befouled streams, raped woodlands, and an atmosphere of fear and hopelessness.

So into the very good creation of God there has come an alien presence, a power of darkness that causes the whole scene to groan, awaiting a deliverance. And the inhabitants are anxious, longing for meaning, for love, for hope. And in their anxiety they keep creating for themselves false saviors and false messiahs.

Is God Angry?

A few years ago a demented young man took a hammer and vandalized Michelangelo's magnificent sculpture, the *Pieta*, in St. Peter's basilica. People who loved art everywhere were incensed that such a piece of art should be defiled thus. Is God angry with the darkness that has come as an alien presence into his creation? We have ceased talking about the "wrath of God" as though we had gotten beyond such a concept in our modernity. Yet it is not difficult from our human perspective to realize that God who created all things very good and who loves deeply, should likewise be angry at the defilement of his expression of himself in his creation. When God's people in Israel, upon whom he had put his love, betrayed his purpose and adopted godless lifestyles, God spoke of his wrath against such wickedness. God's wrath is not the temper tantrum of a petty and vindictive tyrant, but the anger of one who cares very deeply about his own, like a betrayed lover or a disappointed Father.

There are always limitations on trying to explain the response of God to his creation. But the Creator who made all things to function together in harmony with himself and with his *shalom* manifesting itself in all creation is justly angry when his own creation becomes wasted under an alien authority that denies the one who made it all.

And yet God's anger is never wrath as an end in itself. When you're looking at the Bible and reading God's description of this present evil world, as you hear his most serious words of judgment, there keeps stealing through a note of hope, and of expectation. From the early pages of Genesis, the promise of a "seed of woman who shall bruise the serpent's head" gives anticipation that God is going to express his character and purpose in yet another way, by bringing a solution to the problem of evil. But that's for the next chapter.

For now, at least, you have a glimpse of the problem.

CHAPTER 2
The Gospel of
the Kingdom of God

What we want to get at in this chapter is that God invades his creation and establishes his rightful authority; but for that to make sense we have to go back and pick up a few strands. In the last chapter we sketched out the whole idea of the kingdom of darkness to give the backdrop of the biblical message of the kingdom of God. It would be a mistake, however, to assume that God was quiescent until the coming of Jesus. We need to go back to the beginning of scripture and pick up the story of God's involvement with his creation.

But before we do that let me take you on a little side trip!

Belly Button Theology

This is a purposeful bit of foolishness. If you ask a dozen different persons what the Christian faith is, or what the gospel is, you may well get a dozen different answers and all quite correct in their own way. For instance, I can think of many answers I have received:

1. The gospel is being born again.
2. The Christian faith is all about sins being forgiven.
3. The gospel is about salvation.
4. The Christian faith is justification by faith.
5. The gospel is the church and the sacraments.
6. The gospel is liberation for the oppressed.

Each of these is a very real part of the gospel, just as the belly button is a very real part of the physical body. It would be quite easy to see an enlarged photograph of the belly button and to be told that this was the photograph of a human being, and in a real sense that would be a true statement. But as you backed the camera away, more and more of the human body would come into perspective and the belly button would be seen as only a part, though a very real and valid part, of the human body.

Imagine that a person has been in the grips of some moral problem and has been told that Jesus Christ can give the power of a new life, the power to be born again. If he or she experiences that new birth, then the joyous news for that person is being born again. Another person may have been attracted to Jesus Christ and into the community of faith because something in the church and the sacraments provided the key to the meaning of life. For that person the new birth might be an unknown, but church and sacraments would be joyous news.

When I was in school I lived at one point in the gatehouse of the school campus. The campus had at one time been a very large estate of a wealthy sugar manufacturer. Even the small gatehouse was fun to live in, and quite spacious. But it wasn't the whole of the estate. The estate included several gatehouses, stables, formal gardens, servants' quarters; and most prominent was the manor house. The estate was larger than any of these essential parts.

All of this is to establish the point that we dare not minimize the gospel by identifying it with one of its vital facets as though that were the whole thing. This is done so frequently in evangelistic methodology. A person will find that in Jesus Christ the fear of death is removed, or that one is saved not by good works but by faith in Jesus Christ, and will assume that everybody else is looking for that same good news. Or a person will discover that God gives life its perspective and meaning and will develop a whole methodology after that. Praise God for these facets of the gospel! They are all valid. But we need to stand back and look at the whole biblical picture of the gospel and then see how all these are component parts of the magnificently varied grace and power of God.

The Word Gospel

Let's look at the word *gospel* just to be sure we don't have it painted dull gray. With such an overkill of radio and television preachers sternly "preaching the gospel," one fears that it may have a very austere connotation to most ordinary folk. Quite the contrary. It is a word that reflects excited and joyous announcement. But more than that it carries with it the ideas of fulfilled expectation and breathless anticipation. It's the kind of good news you can't keep to yourself. I think immediately of the evening that the announcement came that the Second World War had ended. Our whole lives had been affected by that disaster for several years. I was working that evening in the public library. We had been told by the senior librarian that if the announcement came we could close the library in celebration. When the word came we closed the library and went onto the main street where thousands of people had gathered and were dancing for joy in the street, singing and shouting for sheer gratitude that it was all over. That's gospel. It thrills. It excites. It is full of gratitude and joy.

The word *gospel* comes from a Greek word *euangelion* (meaning "joyous news or announcement"), which comes into English as *evangel,* and the verbal form *evangelism,* or *evangelization.* Given its origin, the word can hardly mean some body of doctrine served up like cold mashed potatoes. Nor can evangelization be properly conceived as some dutiful process of proselyting done to keep the church rolls from showing a decrease in membership. Sadly, it has devolved into this too frequently. No! Evangelism is having such joyous news that it is spontaneously sloshed all over everybody. "We cannot but speak of what we have seen and heard." If you have joyful news, then you are going to have, without premeditation, "joyful new-sing."

The Gospel of the Kingdom

Look now at how this joyful news comes through in the writing of Mark. He begins the account he is writing with the words:

> The beginning of the gospel of Jesus Christ, the Son of God.

So, there you have the word *gospel* used to refer to the person of Jesus Christ. Mark proceeds to tell of the ministry of John the Baptist, of the baptism of Jesus, and then of the time of Jesus' temptation in the wilderness for forty days. But note the drama of the passage that follows (Mark 1:14–15):

> Now after John was arrested, Jesus came into Galilee, preaching the gospel of God, and saying, "The time is fulfilled, and the kingdom of God is at hand; repent, and believe in the gospel."

Here you have the word *gospel* used in two other ways. First, Jesus preaches the good news of God, or God's good news. Then at the end of verse 15 he simply says, "repent and believe the good news."

Let me give you a much freer translation of this same passage and see if we can create some of the vitality which it obviously contains:

> John the Baptist was imprisoned. After that Jesus came into Galilee heralding God's thrilling news. Here's what he said: "The appropriate time has arrived. God's kingdom is near at hand. So get your thinking straight and believe the joyous news."

Do you hear what the joyous news is? On the surface it is a pure political announcement. We have sentimentalized the kingdom of God so much that we have lost the impact of it. A kingdom is a form of government headed by a king or a queen. A kingdom of itself is not necessarily good news. If the king is evil and unjust, then the kingdom can be a nightmare. The character of the kingdom depends on the character of the king. In this instance, Jesus is announcing that God's reign is somehow imminent. What makes this good news is the character of God who is good. It is God who *brings* the good news and God who *is* the good news. His rightful rule in his own creation is somehow at the threshold. Mark's use of the idea "the appropriate time is fulfilled (or, has arrived)" indicates that the kingdom has been expected. This adds to the excitement.

In a kingdom you are dealing primarily with the character and the will of the king. It is this fact that makes the matter of repentance an imperative. One must bring mind and heart into conformity to the mind and heart of the king. If not, you are a disloyal subject, or a downright enemy of the sovereign. The command to repent is followed by the offering of the joyous promise of the kingdom, the good news.

From this beginning, the gospel of the kingdom of God becomes the comprehensive description of the gospel in Matthew, Mark, and Luke. The gospel is referred to in almost no other way. Jesus sends his disciples out to preach the kingdom. He tells parables which begin: "The kingdom of God is like. . . ." He says that the triumphant return of the Lord is dependent upon the gospel of the kingdom being preached to all the nations for a witness.

All of this ought to give us a strong clue as to what the gospel is all about. Even though the Apostle Paul does not use the word or the concept of "the kingdom" a great deal in his writings, it is obviously of utmost significance to him. At the end of the Acts account, we find Paul a prisoner in Rome in his own hired house. And what is he doing for two years? He's teaching the kingdom of God. Can't you imagine that such teaching, if it were widely known, would give the Roman government a case of the "willies"? Imagine, in the seat of world government here is a prisoner saying that the real kingdom has nothing to do with Caesar, but that the true authority is God's, and that God's kingdom is now a fact. That would make Christians a very revolutionary element, as in fact they were (and ought to be still).

Why Was the Kingdom Anticipated?

We Gentiles have a bit of difficulty getting our thinking into the ethos of the first century Jewish community. But the anticipation of the manifest reign of Yahweh (God) was the common property of the Jewish people. It was this anticipation that produced several false messiahs, such was the eagerness to see it come to pass. John the Baptist provoked this anticipation by his preaching and his popularity. So when Jesus came forth publicly talking about God's joyous news, and about the expected time being fulfilled, and about the kingdom being at hand, you can jolly well believe that ears perked up and hearts began to pound with excitement.

What was behind all of this?

Let's go back again to that third chapter of Genesis. The tragedy of the rebellion in the Garden of Eden has taken place. God has announced that there will be dire consequences for Adam and Eve. But right in there is a brief comment by God, which of itself doesn't give much explanation as to what it means, but which indicates that God already has a redemptive plan in view:

> "I will put enmity between you and the woman, and between your seed and her seed; he shall bruise your head, and you shall bruise his heel."   (Gen. 3:15)

What's that all about? No explanation, only a clue that you know is of some significance. Years go by. The world deteriorates. The flood comes in judgment. Things don't look much better. Time goes by again. Then out there in the Middle East, at a time early in the period of recorded human history, God reaches down and touches a God-fearing man named Abram. Abram is probably something like a sheikh, a tribal leader. God makes a promise to him that in his seed all the nations of the earth will be blessed. God makes a number of promises to Abram, changing his name to Abraham and testing him in many ways. But what is significant is that God singles out this one person and makes a promise that has implications for all people.

Abraham, Isaac, Israel. The nation of Israel comes into being

while captive in Egypt. Then come Moses and the Exodus. At
Mount Sinai God tells this peculiar people what they are all
about. He makes a covenant with them. They are to be his own
people. He will be their King. They in turn will be a nation of
priests, to mediate the knowledge of God to all nations. There
are ups and downs. Centuries go by in which Israel experiences
seasons of loyalty and faith, but more often they forget who they
are and who God is.

Again God reaches down and touches a shepherd boy
named David. David is unique in that God's blessing is all over
him. Because David knows who God is, and because he is a
God-fearer and worshiper, he is anointed king of God's people.
God makes a promise to David that his throne shall be estab-
lished *forever.* As we say: "The plot thickens." A woman's seed,
Abraham's seed, now David's throne—all fit somehow into
God's purpose.

But immediately after David things begin to go downhill.
Solomon rules in splendor, but then Rehoboam divides the
kingdom, and from then on it's a sad story. What about David's
"forever throne"? Where is the promise of the kingdom that
shall go on and on? Did God forget?

The Message of the Prophets

A new tack emerges in about the eighth century B.C. God's
people have departed so far from what he covenanted with
them to be that he sends prophets to remind them of who they
are and why they are. The prophets have a primary responsibility to call the people of God to remember the covenant and its
provisions. God promised that as his people lived out their lives
in response to his will he would bless them beyond imagining.
But if they ceased to respond to him in obedience to his purpose
there would be some very severe consequences—judgment.

You can see that God's will is not arbitrary. God acts out of
his own character. God expresses himself in harmony with who
he is. His people were to be a holy nation in that they also were
to act out, or demonstrate to the world, who God is and what

God's will is all about. Only in that way would they be a blessing to the earth. In the strong prophetic statements from God's spokesmen you get a very good picture of what God is like.

Take Isaiah, for instance. He was speaking to people who had religion aplenty. They had all the trappings of temple, priests, and sacrifices. They were offering up endless sacrifices and going through ritual fastings, but it was all facade. Their ethics were abominable. Their personal lives were petty and dishonest and oppressive. You see something of the character and will of God when he speaks to them through Isaiah and says:

> "Is not this the fast that I choose:
>   to loose the bonds of wickedness,
>   to undo the thongs of the yoke,
> to let the oppressed go free,
>   and to break every yoke?
> Is it not to share your bread with the hungry,
>   and to bring the homeless poor into your house;
> when you see the naked, to cover him,
>   and not to hide yourself from your own flesh?
> Then shall your light break forth like the dawn,
>   and your healing shall spring up speedily;
> your righteousness shall go before you,
>   the glory of the LORD shall be your rear guard.
> Then you shall call, and the LORD will answer;
>   you shall cry, and he will say, Here I am.
> "If you take away from the midst of you the yoke,
>   the pointing of the finger, and the speaking wickedness,
> if you pour yourself out for the hungry
>   and satisfy the desire of the afflicted,
> then shall your light rise in the darkness
>   and your gloom be as the noonday."
>
> (Isa. 58:6–10)

In a subsequent passage, which Jesus later would quote as referring to himself, we get a similar insight into the heart of God:

> The Spirit of the Lord GOD is upon me,
>   because the LORD has anointed me
> to bring good tidings to the afflicted;
>   he has sent me to bind up the brokenhearted,

> to proclaim liberty to the captives,
>> and the opening of the prison to those who are bound;
> to proclaim the year of the LORD's favor,
>> and the day of vengeance of our God;
>> to comfort all who mourn;
> to grant to those who mourn in Zion—
>> to give them a garland instead of ashes,
> the oil of gladness instead of mourning,
>> the mantle of praise instead of a faint spirit;
> that they may be called oaks of righteousness,
>> the planting of the LORD, that he may be glorified.
>>   (Isa. 61:1–3)

This was no new message. This was all in the covenant. God's people were to have been living out their relation to God in this kind of ethical response all along. In these passages especially we see God's compassionate regard for the hapless victims of the kingdom of darkness: the hungry, the homeless, the naked, the afflicted, the mourning, the imprisoned, and the despairing.

Because these people had broken the covenant and profaned the sabbaths, God was, true to his word, about to bring upon them a disaster. This announcement of the disaster was also the function of the prophets. Both Israel (the Northern Kingdom) and Judah (the Southern Kingdom) were soon taken captive by the great empires of the day. The judgment came with devastating certainty.

The prophets had another function, however, and that was to speak the word of hope, of that which was yet to be. In the midst of the most awesome statements of God's displeasure with his people will come these words of hope to the effect that God is not forgetting his covenant, or his people. Such words will deal with God's intention to forgive his people's sin:

> ". . . I will forgive their iniquity, and I will remember their sin no more."   (Jer. 31:34)

Or they will speak of a new covenant:

> "Behold, the days are coming, says the LORD, when I will make a new covenant with the house of Israel and the house of Judah, . . . I will put my law within them, and

> I will write it upon their hearts; and I will be their God,
> and they shall be my people."   (Jer. 31:31,33)

From the midst of all these words of hope, the very clear idea keeps emerging that a special person, an anointed person, is coming to implement the will of God:

> For to us a child is born,
>   to us a son is given;
> and the government will be upon his shoulder,
>   and his name will be called
> "Wonderful Counselor, Mighty God, Everlasting Father,
>   Prince of Peace."
> Of the increase of his government and of peace
>   there will be no end,
> upon the throne of David, and over his kingdom,
>   to establish it, and to uphold it
> with justice and with righteousness
>   from this time forth and for evermore.
> The zeal of the LORD of hosts will do this.   (Isa. 9:6–7)

There are so many faces given to this anointed person, or messiah, it is no wonder that when he came people didn't know exactly what he would be like. He was to be: king, deliverer, healer, servant, and sin-bearer. He was to be a prophet. He was to be a different kind of priest, and much more. But in all of these prophecies the notion of the seed of Abraham who would bring blessing began to take on character, as the beleagured people of God waited.

In the later pre-Christian centuries there emerged the teaching of the *malkuth shamaim,* the coming manifest reign of Yahweh (God). Every Hebrew child was taught by the rabbi of the *malkuth shamaim.* All Hebrews had this expectation deeply ingrained in their consciousness. In our Christian tradition we sense this expectation in the Advent hymns:

> O come, O come, Emmanuel,
> And ransom captive Israel,
> That mourns in lonely exile here
> Until the Son of God appear.
> Rejoice! Rejoice! Emmanuel
> Shall come to thee, O Israel.

You really need to have in your bones this feeling of anticipation, which belonged to the Jewish people, to appreciate the
high drama that reveals itself in the early pages of the New
Testament. The atmosphere of expectation hung in the very air
of Israel through all the tragedy of occupation, first by the
Greeks, and then by the Romans. God would surely come.

Advent

And come he did!

God invades human history. An angel comes to a devout
peasant girl with this announcement:

> "Hail, O favored one, the Lord is with you! . . . Do not
> be afraid, Mary, for you have found favor with God. And
> behold, you will conceive in your womb and bear a son,
> and you shall call his name Jesus."

(Now, pay close attention to the content of what follows.)

> "He will be great, and will be called the Son of the Most
>   High;
> and the Lord God will give to him the throne of his father
>   David,
> and he will reign over the house of Jacob for ever;
> and of his kingdom there will be no end."
>
>   (Luke 1:28, 30–32)

The Son of the Most High. The throne of David. The unending
kingdom. There it is!

When Mary sings her song of praise, which we call the Mag-
nificat, she dwells on the fact that God is going to show himself
strong on behalf of the poor, the weak, the oppressed, and the
godly. The rich, the proud, and the mighty will come off poorly.
When we are thinking of gospel and of salvation we must of
necessity feed in this kind of biblical content to get a proper
concept of the content of New Testament faith. It is pretty
radical stuff.

To the shepherds the angels give the announcement in no
uncertain terms: "Behold, I bring you good news of a great joy
which will come to all the people; for to you is born this day in

the city of David a Savior, who is Christ (Messiah) the Lord"
(Luke 2:10–11). So the baby is born.

Don't forget Simeon, either. Simeon was a devout soul who
had been waiting in the temple because it had been revealed
to him that he would not die until he had seen the Lord's Christ.
And when Jesus is brought to the temple for purification,
Simeon says that which we now call the *Nunc Dimittis:*

> "Lord, now lettest thou thy servant depart in peace,
> according to thy word;
> for mine eyes have seen thy salvation
> which thou hast prepared in the presence of all peoples,
> a light for revelation to the Gentiles,
> and for glory to thy people Israel."
>
> (Luke 2:29–32)

There are a couple of things in Simeon's prayer that we need
to register. First, he uses the word "salvation" in its majestic
biblical sense, in its broad meaning of God come to make all
things right and new. I underscore that because, in evangelical
circles, we all too often have a habit of speaking of salvation in
very individual and narrow ways. Secondly, Simeon speaks of
salvation as being for all peoples, even the Gentiles. This was a
valid concern from the scriptures of the Hebrews, but they had
forgotten it and had become very provincial in their thinking.

All the designations of this child are fraught with meaning:
Jesus—Yahweh who saves; *Emmanuel*—God with us; *Christ*—
Anointed One; and *Lord*—he is in fact God. Here he is, then,
perfect God and perfect man. The King has come!

The Kingdom of God Is at Hand

The drama of all of this makes you break out in gooseflesh.
And nowhere more than in the first chapter of Mark, which we
quoted earlier. "The appropriate moment has arrived. The
kingdom of God is at hand. Get your mind and heart together
with that of the King, and believe the joyous news."

Shortly after his baptism Jesus comes to Nazareth and into
the synagogue on the sabbath. In a moment of high drama he

is given the scroll of the prophet Isaiah, and reads publicly the passage:

> "The Spirit of the Lord is upon me,
> because he has anointed me to preach good news to the
>   poor.
> He has sent me to proclaim release to the captives
> and recovering of sight to the blind,
> to set at liberty those who are oppressed,
> to proclaim the acceptable year of the Lord."
>
> (Luke 4:18–19)

Now look what follows. He hands the scroll back to the attendant, and all the eyes in the synagogue are looking at him; with utter candor he asserts: "Today this scripture has been fulfilled in your hearing." Wow! He claims the fulfillment of that prophecy from Isaiah in himself.

In the present-day Christian scene we have focused so primarily on the issues of sin, guilt, and forgiveness that we have tended to obscure these other signs of the kingdom that Jesus speaks of. After all, the signs of the kingdom are the signs that bespeak the character and will of the Lord.

As if the passage in Luke 4 were not sufficient, there is another very dramatic statement of the signs of the kingdom that Jesus uses to proclaim his messianic role. That other passage is on the occasion that the imprisoned John the Baptist has some misgivings about whether Jesus is really the one they had looked for to be messiah. He sends disciples to ask Jesus pointedly.

Jesus' answer might well go right over the heads of those of us who are Gentiles by heritage, but to any Hebrew schooled in the scriptures it speaks of the signs of the kingdom. Jesus doesn't answer John directly. He simply rehearses the signs. He says to the disciples of John:

> "Go and tell John what you hear and see: the blind receive their sight and the lame walk, lepers are cleansed and the deaf hear, and the dead are raised up, and the poor have good news preached to them. And blessed is he who takes no offense at me."   (Matt. 11: 4–6)

The kingdom of God is not just heralded in words but in the deeds that are the signs of the kingdom. This principle remains true today.

One sobering reminder of this requirement to live out the kingdom signs is found in Matthew 25. Jesus is speaking of the day when he returns as Lord of Glory. He will summon the nations before him and judge them upon the basis of their having done those works that are signs of his divine will and character: feeding the hungry, giving drink to the thirsty, taking the homeless into our homes, clothing the naked, and ministering to the sick and imprisoned. This kind of life is very much at the heart of his kingdom. We will come back to that.

The theme of Jesus' evangelizing ministry was the kingdom of God. That is the comprehensive theme we must lay hold of to give our efforts their true New Testament flavor. The demand of the kingdom is that we must repent and come to terms with the Lord. The promises are that the Lord welcomes the helpless, the penitent, those who come to him in love and trust.

Kingdom evangelism has a thoughtful understanding of the nature of the kingdom of God and of how that kingdom is joyous news. Here is a definition that you will find helpful:

> This "kingdom," in biblical usage, refers not primarily to the divine sovereignty in a general sense, but to the active, saving reign of the Triune God in history. The coming kingdom is not static but dynamic, not so much a concept as a ruling power. To proclaim "the kingdom of God has drawn near" is to herald those mighty events in which God's royal rule has invaded the earth in the coming of Jesus Christ and in the power of the Holy Spirit. It is to bring the thrilling news of God's victory in the death and resurrection of His Son over all the dark powers that have enslaved mankind and made His good creation subject to bondage. It is to tell of what God has done to bring forgiveness to the guilty, help to the poor, release to the captives, sight to the blind, deliverance to the oppressed. It is to announce to the whole creation a divine reign of justice and peace.[1]

Right into the middle of the dominion of darkness comes the invasion of God, the light, in the person of Jesus Christ. And Jesus inaugurates the kingdom of God. The King has come. The Word of God is made flesh. The light shines in the darkness. The age to come invades this present age. Jesus also announces that there will come a "day" at the "end" when the kingdom will be consummated and every foe will be eliminated. Meanwhile, the kingdom is dynamically present, the reign of God is active among us. So we pray for the increasing manifestation of that reign in the Lord's Prayer: "Let your kingdom come actually and completely."

To quote again from the *Evangelism Manifesto:*

> Together with this grand announcement, the proclamation of the kingdom brings a summons. Hearers are called to renounce all sin, each false lord, every rival sovereignty, and to submit through repentance and faith to God's saving reign in Christ. The proclamation demands commitment to God's lordship and obedience to His will in the world. Although the decisive victory over the forces of evil has been won, the conflict still rages. Christ is risen; the Spirit has been poured out upon the church; the powers of the coming age are at work in the world, but the end is not yet. Hosts of darkness resist God's sovereignty; rampant evils oppose His will. To repent and believe is to side with God's purpose in this conflict—assured of ultimate victory, while contending God's righteousness in every sphere of life.[2]

The focus of the gospel of the kingdom is the King, the sovereign Lord God. The King is manifest in Jesus Christ. He is Lord! The nature of the kingdom is that it is joyous news. It is the expression of the character and purpose of God in bringing peace to those with whom he is well pleased.

Let's Return to Act Two

You will remember that in the last chapter we were thinking in terms of the drama of creation and the rebellion. Act one closed with the apparent triumph of darkness, except for that final word of hope and the musical note of joy which fed into the dissonant orchestration. Now the curtain rises on act two. In scene after scene the word of the gracious Creator breaks into the darkness and silence with increasing insistence. As one reflects on what is transpiring it is obvious that the Creator has not forsaken his creation but in many ways is at work to keep it from destroying itself. He even provides people with the skills to make life humane and beautiful.

The darkness is real. The tragic is apparent. But that promise of redemption which came in softly at the close of act one, begins to be more explicit and more intriguing as it comes to Abraham, to David, and to the prophets. As the promise comes in scene after scene in the time of preparation, so that joyous and harmonious theme gains intensity in the orchestration, in demanding counterpoint to the dissonant and discordant theme of the dominion of darkness. As the human situation seems more and more hopeless, the expectancy of the divine promise "stirs on the earth and trembles in the air." And so act two comes to a close, with centuries of silence, and darkness— and hope.

Act Three, the Advent and the Inauguration

Now get the scenario. Right into the midst of the dominion of darkness—with all of the tragic, with all of the discordant themes that are part of that dominion—right into the midst of that comes the "seed of the woman." It is with this event that act three opens. The redemption theme soars in the orchestra. The light has come.

The sheer drama of act three is not to be taken for granted. This seed of the woman is no less than the Creator come into his own creation. And he has come to claim his own. God comes in person, in the person of Jesus Christ. What is his purpose in coming? To inaugurate his own kingdom which is forever. So we have a clash of dominions! And what is the future of the dominion of darkness? Well, act three is still in progress, but there are some things that we know from our King. With the coming of the Incarnate Word of God we also get the explanation of many mysteries, one of which is the final destiny of all the forces of evil. We are told that the two kingdoms, or domains, will coexist in conflict until the "day" or the "end" when the exalted Lord Jesus returns:

> Then comes the end, when he delivers the kingdom to God the Father after destroying every rule and every authority and power. For he must reign until he has put all his enemies under his feet. . . . When all things are subjected to him, then the Son himself will also be subjected to him who put all things under him, that God may be everything to every one.
>
> (1 Cor. 15:24, 25, 28)

In this ongoing drama, then, we know that act three will continue through "this age." During this period God's kingdom people will be in continual conflict with darkness, as they express their loyalty to the Creator and as they bear the joyous news of his forever kingdom to the inhabitants and to the structures of this present world. But the final act is going to begin when Jesus has "destroyed every rule and power," when his kingdom is consummated at his glorious return. Act four will begin at the second advent of Jesus Christ. We, then, are part of the exciting drama of act three, and looking for act four.

Jesus and the New Testament writers speak of the kingdom of God in three different tenses: as having already come, as now present, and as yet to come. Other Christians today speak of the "already-but-not-yet kingdom." When Jesus the Lord came he did in fact come to inaugurate his kingdom. That is his first advent. At the present time we are between the ages in the sense that while this present age is still with us, the age to come has come upon us so that the kingdom of God is dynamically present. But the kingdom is not consummated until Jesus returns in power and great glory at the second advent.

This understanding is critical for wholesome discipleship. It gives us a sense of history, of calling and identity, of purpose and ultimate triumph.

We will be coming back to the "between the ages" period,

which is where we live and where our evangelism and Christian community take place. That's another whole exciting area of exploration. But for now we need to spend a chapter looking more closely at the first advent of God in Jesus Christ.

CHAPTER 3
The Gospel of the Glory of Christ

> And even if our gospel is veiled, it is veiled only to those who are perishing. In their case the god of this world has blinded the minds of the unbelievers, to keep them from seeing the light of the gospel of the glory of Christ, who is the likeness of God.
>
> (2 Cor. 4:3–4)

This very provocative passage illumines some of the conflict we are engaged in as we present Jesus Christ to people. It also offers a necessary clue to the person of Jesus Christ. And the gospel is identified here as the gospel of the glory of Christ. Having spent some considerable space getting to the point of Jesus' role as the King, I feel we must stop and look at him and absorb some more of the biblical flavor of who this person "beyond imagining" is.

To say that Jesus of Nazareth is the kingly Messiah and the hope of Israel is to say that Jesus Christ is Lord. He is identified as the Anointed One of God (Yahweh) and the divine Sovereign as well as the person Jesus. The idea of lordship, or sovereignty, was paramount in the teaching of the early church. "Jesus is Lord" is the most elemental and earliest profession of faith. There is also no question that the major theme of Jesus' preaching and that of his disciples was the kingdom of God and the joyous and demanding implications of that kingdom.

But that's not all!

Anyone who is at all conversant with the content of the Bible knows that Jesus' kingly reign is not the only face on his advent.

The longer one looks at the scriptures pertaining to Jesus Christ, the more one is compelled to bow in adoration and worship. Charles Wesley, the hymn writer, fittingly speaks of casting our crowns before him, "lost in wonder, love, and praise." Yes, this is the only adequate response to who he is. The longer you look, the more you are overwhelmed at the marvel of his person and his work. In C. S. Lewis's delightful allegory, *The Chronicles of Narnia,* the Christ-figure is Aslan, the lion. It is a common understanding of those who know Aslan that the more you look at him, the larger he becomes.

In Revelation Jesus is also figured as a lion, only in a fashion that thrills and staggers the imagination. And that brings us to the point of this chapter. The writer of Revelation is shown the scroll that contains the mysteries of history and of redemption, and he weeps that no one is able to open it.

> Then one of the elders said to me, "Weep not; lo, the Lion of the tribe of Judah, the Root of David, has conquered, so that he can open the scroll and its seven seals."
> And between the throne and the four living creatures and among the elders, I saw a Lamb standing, as though it had been slain. . . .
>
> (Rev. 5:5–6)

The majestic lion, figuring strength and authority, appears as, of all things, a lamb having been slain. And as John, the writer, looks, the assembled elders sing a new song:

> "Worthy art thou to take the scroll and to open its seals, for thou wast slain and by thy blood didst ransom men for God
> from every tribe and tongue and people and nation, and hast made them a kingdom and priests to our God, and they shall reign on earth."
>
> (Rev. 5:9–10)

Who but God would have ever conceived such? Jesus, the kingly Messiah, is also the Lamb of God who takes away the sins of the world. You cannot isolate or disconnect these complementary themes in the New Testament. John the Baptist announces: "Behold, the Lamb of God, who takes away the sin of the world!" From heaven comes the affirmation of the Father: "Thou art my beloved Son; with thee I am well pleased." Eternal Son, and Lamb slain from the foundation of the world! His death on the cross for our sins is so paramount in the mind of Paul that he can say, "I decided to know nothing among you except Jesus Christ and him crucified" (1 Cor. 2:2). The cross is not by accident the great symbol of our Christian faith.

Suffering Servant

In the Philippian letter, Paul ties Christ's deity, his humbling, his death, and his exaltation all together:

> ... Christ Jesus, who, though he was in the form of God, did not count equality with God a thing to be grasped, but emptied himself, taking the form of a servant, being born in the likeness of men. And being found in human form he humbled himself and became obedient unto death, even death on a cross. Therefore God has highly exalted him and bestowed on him the name which is above every name, that at the name of Jesus every knee should bow, in heaven and on earth and under the earth, and every tongue confess that Jesus Christ is Lord, to the glory of God the Father.   (Phil. 2:5–11)

The concept of the servant of Yahweh who suffers for the sins of the people of Yahweh comes through very clearly in the prophet Isaiah (Isa. 53). Jesus himself was quite candid about the fact that he had to suffer and to be executed. He was quite conscious of the fact that he had come for such a purpose. And the reason behind all of this is that God is providing a redemption from the consequences of the darkness in his own typically marvelous way. To explore this idea is enough for volumes in itself.

Great High Priest

The writer of Hebrews sets forth Jesus as our great high priest, who is not only a perfect and compassionate high priest because he has taken our nature, but also is the tabernacle, and also is the sacrifice. As a matter of fact, the writer states that we are not really mature Christians until we grasp the reality of Christ's high priestly ministry. That particular letter depends very much on an adequate understanding of the Jewish sacrificial system. It is always necessary to take a group of Gentile Christians back and run them through Leviticus to give them the flavor.

Jesus comes as the great consummation of the sacrificial system and offers a perfect, once-for-all sacrifice, in contrast to the year-by-year sacrifices of Judaism. Because the Old Testament priests were imperfect, and because the sacrifices had to be repeated year by year, they were obviously lacking in perfection and thus could not free the conscience of the effects of sin. The writer of Hebrews pursues the point that because Jesus is a perfect high priest, he offers a perfect sacrifice (himself). Now as priest he intercedes for us at the right hand of God in the perfect tabernacle and on the basis of his own blood. Because of this, the guilt, the power, and the conscience of sin are all dealt with so that we may, with perfect freedom, worship the living God. Hallelujah!

When the New Testament calls Jesus *Savior* it is indicating that he saves us as individuals from the guilt and disastrous consequences of sin, but it is also saying much, much more. He has come to effect a regeneration, to institute a new creation, a kingdom wherein are righteousness, peace, and joy in the Holy Spirit. There is a cosmic and communal as well as an individual and personal implication of his role as Savior!

A Montage of Roles and Descriptions

I saw a poster some months ago on which all the names and titles of Jesus were incorporated on a very colorful graphic. For the sake of our discussion here let me just run by you in random fashion a number of the roles and descriptions attributed to the person Jesus Christ. You will find that they form a montage that makes him ever larger in your conception of who he is, and of what he has done and continues to do.

Jesus is the *personification of the infinite and unimaginable love of God* for his rebel creation. Paul prays for the Ephesian Christians that they "may have power to comprehend with all the saints what is the breadth and length and height and depth, and to know the love of Christ which surpasses knowledge . . ." (Eph. 3:18–19). In this amazing act of grace the offended Creator comes to the offending creature, the righteous to the guilty, with an offer of clemency, love, and adoption into the family of God.

Jesus is *that one by whom we understand grace.* There is nothing that merits such an offer as God makes to us in Christ. John records that "the law was given through Moses," but "grace and truth came through Jesus Christ" (John 1:17). Such love cannot be earned. Paul exults in the fact that because we are declared righteous by faith we have peace with God through our Lord Jesus Christ, and through him have obtained access to this grace in which we stand (Rom. 5:1–2). Grace has made us free. The kingdom of God is a kingdom of grace. "In him [Christ] we have," says Paul, "redemption through his blood, the forgiveness of our trespasses, according to the riches of his grace" (Eph. 1:7). Jesus is God's gift (grace) to us, and in him God richly graces us with all that we need to be the heirs of eternal salvation.

Jesus comes *to give life and to give it abundantly.* To those who have dwelt in the domain of darkness, in spiritual death, in the servitude to sin, comes one who provides joyous, free, purposeful life.

Akin to that is the fact that Jesus, by tasting death for everyone and by rising triumphant over death and the grave, *has conquered death.* Death is no longer the enemy. Death has lost its sting. The grave has lost its victory. And those persons who were all their lifetimes held captive by the fear of death have been delivered by the Easter triumph. The anxiety over death is one of the most common human anxieties, and to that anxiety Jesus says: "I am the resurrection and the life; he who believes in me, though he die, yet shall he live" (John 11:25).

We, by faith, become *sharers in his resurrection life*. Eternal life is the life of the age to come that becomes ours by the Holy Spirit. In a mind-boggling statement, Paul says that the Spirit that raised Jesus from the dead is the same Spirit that dwells in our mortal bodies (Rom. 8:11). Because he has been raised from the dead by the glory of the Father, we too walk in newness of life (Rom. 6:4).

Jesus is the *friend of sinners*. His enemies thought this accusation would so scar his reputation that he would be destroyed. But think what it does for the likes of us! He responded to his accusers that it is not the folks who are healthy who need a physician, but those who are sick, and that he did not come to call the righteous, but sinners. So there! If we were righteous we wouldn't need a savior. But we aren't! We're real sinners. And for Jesus to be called the friend of sinners means that we can come to him knowing full well that he understands exactly what we are like. One of Paul's most heartwarming passages echoes this theme:

> While we were yet helpless, at the right time Christ died for the ungodly. Why, one will hardly die for a righteous man—though perhaps for a good man one will dare even to die. But God shows his love for us in that while we were yet sinners Christ died for us. Since, therefore, we are now justified by his blood, much more shall we be saved by him from the wrath of God. For if while we were enemies we were reconciled to God by the death of his Son, much more, now that we are reconciled, shall we be saved by his life.   (Rom. 5:6–10)

The gospel that Jesus is the friend of sinners continues to come with new waves of meaning as we move on in our Christian life and discover new depths of sin and need. And John reminds us that Jesus is no less the friend of sinners now than he was at the time when he first called us to himself:

> If we say we have no sin, we deceive ourselves, and the truth is not in us. If we confess our sins, he is faithful and just, and will forgive our sins and cleanse us from all unrighteousness.   (1 John 1:8–9)

Jesus is *true man,* or true humanity. He is paradigm man. As the scriptures state, he did not take on himself the form of angels, but took on himself the seed of Abraham and became like us in every way. He is touched with the feeling of our infirmity and tempted in all points as we are. He is called the second Adam. He is the beginning of the new covenant humanity. He demonstrates what our humanity is all about.

He is also *God.* By his own words, "He who has seen me has seen the Father; I and the Father are one" (John 14:9; 10:30). Or as the prologue to the letter to the Hebrew Christians states it: "He reflects the glory of God and bears the very stamp of his nature, upholding the universe by his word of power" (Heb. 1:3).

This remains one of the great mysteries of the Christian faith: how Jesus can be truly God and truly man at once. Church councils have labored long over how to assure that both natures are properly stated in our creeds. The twin questions recur again and again: Can this one, so obviously human, also be divine? And can one who is so manifestly God be, at the same time, human? But the church in its simplest creed links the human name "Jesus" with the affirmation of deity, "Lord," and says that both are true, "Jesus is Lord!"

Jesus is then *the answer to the most profound questions of life.* He speaks to the meaning of life, to our acceptance with God, and to the mystery of death. And the answer is himself. "I am the way, the truth, and the life." When the Christians at Colossae got their feet tangled up in Greek philosophies that posited a whole ascending array of semi-gods on up to some transcendent super-god and were tempted to put Jesus in the chain somewhere, Paul wrote one of the breathtaking philosophical statements in scripture:

> He [Jesus] is the image of the invisible God, the first-born of all creation; for in him all things were created, in heaven and on earth, visible and invisible, whether thrones or dominions or principalities or authorities—all things were created through him and for him. He is before all things, and in him all things hold together. He is

the head of the body, the church; he is the beginning, the first-born from the dead, that in everything he might be pre-eminent. For in him all the fulness of God was pleased to dwell, and through him to reconcile to himself all things, whether on earth or in heaven, making peace by the blood of his cross.   (Col. 1:15–20)

And this is only the beginning. There is so much more that could be said. I only want to establish the fact that the focus of the gospel of the kingdom is on the King, Jesus the Lord, but that he is also the one who redeems us by his blood unto God. The Lion is also the Lamb!

The gospel of the glory of Christ! I struggle with the concept of glory. Properly it has several shades of meaning, depending on its usage. It can refer to a splendor or a sublimity, or to something that is reflective of or that dwells with that splendor. But that definition doesn't help me get my hands on the concept. Let me put together a homemade meaning that is helpful to me and which fits the language. God's glory is his expression of himself, of his being. His works of creation are expressive of his glory as they express his creative will. His people glorify him as they reflect who he is and as they demonstrate his will and character. But the glory of God is most clearly seen as God shows himself in his own Son. "We have beheld his glory, glory as of the only Son from the Father" (John 1:14).

The joyous news we have in Jesus Christ is the joyous news of God making known what he is like, how he loves, what his purpose is to his rebel creation, to what extent he is willing to go to redeem and to bring back into living relationship with himself that which is his own by right of creation.

In Jesus God comes into our humanity and we behold his glory, we see what he is like, and it is joyous news!

CHAPTER 4

The Kingdom Between the Ages: Holiness as a Sign

Let me huff and puff and see if I can blow away some of the fog that continues to surround the concept of the kingdom of God, which is our joyous news, in the Christian community. The fog has to do with a very common notion that we don't have to give much thought to the kingdom of God at the present, but that we wait until Jesus comes again and he will set up his kingdom. The fog is evident in the bumper stickers one sees around that announce "THE KING IS COMING." Now that certainly is true according to our biblical faith. But I always have the mischievous desire to pull alongside those cars with the bumper sticker, roll down my window, and ask: "Say, did you know the King has already come?"

You see, we have gotten into some habits within our Christian community that betray a certain mindlessness concerning what we are about. We can talk easily (in some circles) about being saved, without ever understanding saved from what? or to what? Or we can talk about joining the church without any concept of how that relates to Jesus or his kingdom. The idea of Christian calling, likewise, can devolve into something like a vocational choice. So it is not even valid to begin to think about substantial New Testament evangelism until we have some legitimate concept of who we are, why we are here, and what all of this has to do with the very thing Jesus heralded with such joy, namely the kingdom of God!

For if our calling is out of the dominion of darkness and into the kingdom of God, then what we are called into is obviously a whole new way of life with character and discipline. The Lord certainly did not offer his Son to bring the forgiveness of our sins just so that we could go out and do the same things all over again. Nor was it his design that we should be called his children and yet be indistinguishable from the children of darkness. If the kingdom is like a nobleman going into a far country who entrusts his financial affairs to several stewards who are responsible to that nobleman for the increase of the finances when he returns (Luke 19:11 ff.)—then you and I have a very well-defined stewardship as those to whom the affairs of the kingdom are entrusted. We are not, like the wicked servant in the parable, to bury the money in the ground out of timidity, but rather to take risks so that our Lord will receive with increase when he returns. Behind that parable is quite obviously the fact that the King who has come has an agenda: the honor of his name, the increase of his dominion, and the implementation of his gracious will.

Back to the bumper sticker. What concerns us as Christians is that the Lord has come. He has inaugurated his kingom. He has spoken and given us the message of the kingdom and of the will of the King, and, in the figure of the parable, he has gone into a far country. We are answerable upon his return for how we have obeyed the gospel, for our obedience of faith. When the disciples were with Jesus immediately before his ascension, they were asking him about the restoration of the kingdom to Israel. They were still expecting an immediate temporal rulership in splendor that would throw off the yoke of Rome and all of that. Jesus tells them, almost abruptly, that their responsibility is to obey their commission, so to get with it. The kingdom of God will be consummated in power and great glory at the advent of Christ's return. But our attention needs to be focused with earnestness on the agenda of that kingdom which is very really present, with that "age to come" which has intruded into the present in Jesus Christ. The name, the kingdom, and the will of our King are what are to be occupying us until he comes.

What are the signs of the kingdom of God? What evidence is there of the King and his rule? What are the signs of the age to come? What does the world see? What do people see that stands out in evident contrast to this age that gives them a clue about the reality of the King and the kingdom? How do you incite curiosity and inquiry about the kingdom? How do you demonstrate the reality of the kingdom, and allegiance to the King? These are the kinds of questions we need to be asking.

But, given our present mentality, these questions don't make much sense! The common assumption today is that Jesus is the founder of another religion. There are even Christian people who think that Jesus came to provide a much better religion for the world, though not to disturb sincere believers of the other valid religions! Would you believe that? It's true.

Here's what we need to get very clear from the New Testament: *Religion* is tame, polite, safe, and usually respectable—*but Jesus isn't!* Jesus came with an absolute claim. Jesus came as a counterrevolutionary in the best sense of the word. He came as rightful sovereign into his own creation, which was under the domain of an alien authority. He came to bring about a whole new order. And he promised that he would be disruptive, and that to follow him would bring tribulation.

With that in mind, the question of how to incite curiosity and inquiry about the kingdom sounds like the old riddle: How do you hide an elephant? The question is not, How do you incite curiosity and inquiry? but rather, How do you hide a revolution? Do you see the point I'm trying to make? To think in terms of how we might catch the attention of the society in which we live so that we might politely share with them about our religion is to miss the radical nature of our gospel. Jesus is the true radical, and those who are convinced of him become likewise a radical people. As Jesus is both Lord and example, his people have the same devotion to the new order; they have the same way of thinking and behaving. In one way, that makes them, to use St. Francis's expression, "instruments of his peace"; but in another way, that makes Christ's people troublesome. That troublesomeness is not cantankerousness, but redemptive assertion of the values of the kingdom. We may be committed to being good citizens, but we will not call Caesar "Lord"!

In a lighter vein, F. R. Maltby has given us the maxim that Jesus promised his followers three things: that "they would be absurdly happy, completely fearless, and in constant trouble."[3] You see, if "sin" is that prevailing power and lifestyle that denies God, for all practical purposes, in thinking, values, allegiances, and goals—then to yield ourselves to the Lordship of the Son of God brings us into an immediate conflict. And though some cultures and societies reflect the cultural influence of the kingdom of God more than others, the kingdoms of this world have not yet become "the kingdoms of our God and of his Christ."

Let's Reclaim the Designation: Holiness

Let me define *holiness* with one of my homemade definitions. *Holiness* is one of those very common biblical words that almost nobody can give you a good "down home" definition for. Yet the scriptures teach that without holiness no person shall see God (Heb. 12:14). When used of the characteristics of God, such as "holy love," it is an adjective of adjectives and pertains to the infinitely perfect characteristics of God, and to the fact that all his characteristics are in harmony with one another. He is not a dis-integrated God. His perfections are all in a relationship of harmony with each other. Love and wrath, transcendence and immanence, are all attributes of a holy God. He is not at odds with himself.

When we are called to be holy what we are talking about is something like being, or living, in a relationship of integrity and harmony with the will and character of our King and Father. It is a call to flesh out the family likeness of God's family, to demonstrate the lifestyle of God's new covenant humanity.

> As obedient children, do not be conformed to the passions of your former ignorance, but as he who called you is holy, be holy yourselves in all your conduct. . . .
> (1 Pet. 1:14–15)

It has been our tendency to avoid, if not eschew, the idea of being holy, as though it betrayed some kind of offensive pretentiousness of piety. Yet it is our calling and we need to boldly reclaim it in all of its wholesome biblical integrity.

Holiness and repentance go hand in hand. When Jesus came preaching the kingdom of God and calling persons to repentance and faith, he was calling them to a transformation of their way of looking at the world and at life. He was calling them to a radical new outlook that would be determined by who he is and by his absolute claim. The Greek word for repentance has to do with a transformation of mind. It is through this transformation of mind that the Christian person is created more and more in holiness; that is, it is through this discipline of repentance that the Christian comes into a dynamic harmony with the character and will of the Lord, the King.

Different Christian writers deal with this whole concern using different figures. One says that by the end of the century, all of us Christians will be known as "holies" because of our different lives. Another says that we Christians must become what he calls a "cognitive deviant minority." What he is suggesting is that we must self-consciously be at odds with the milieu of darkness. Still another says we must become a Christian counterculture, expressive of the Sermon on the Mount (we'll come back to that). And another calls for a "third race," i.e., a revolutionary race of Christians that set themselves against the cultural tides as expressive of the new creation, as the joyous people of the kingdom of God.

However one expresses it, we desperately need to realize who we are (the people of the King), where we are (between the ages), what we are called to be about (light in the darkness), and where we are going (to that time when the kingdoms of this world become the kingdom of our God and of his Christ). Nowhere does this come out in more graphic statement than in Paul's word:

> I appeal to you therefore, brethren, by the mercies of God, to present your bodies as a living sacrifice, holy and acceptable to God, which is your spiritual worship. Do not be conformed to this world but be transformed by the renewal of your mind, that you may prove what is the will of God, what is good and acceptable and perfect.
> (Rom. 12:1–2)

The use of the word "prove" says to us that between the ages
we are the very demonstration of what God is about—or even
more, of what God is like. A brief look at some scriptures will
give us a clue as to what that looks like.

Slaves of Sin, or Slaves of Righteousness

Part of our current problem is that we have served up a "no
offense" notion of Christian faith that is marketable without
mentioning the costly demands of the gospel of the kingdom of
God. But see how radical is the demand that is basic to the New
Testament picture of Christian faith. Look at the sixth chapter
of Romans. Right off the writer disavows that a Christian can be
at all casual about sin or even entertain the idea that such a
lifestyle is compatible with those who belong to Jesus Christ.
And why so? Because our very baptism is our rite of identification with a real death to sin. We are baptized *into* Jesus Christ,
and into his death, whereby the power and guilt of sin were
borne on the cross for us. It is unthinkable that we should be so
self-contradictory as to think that we could at once live in that
unto which we have died! So, he presses the point, we must go
on always considering ourselves to be dead to sin but alive to
Jesus Christ.

In very practical ways, then, the values, fashions, systems of
unrighteousness, empty causes, and destructive passions must
always be recognized for what they are, as unholy, and must be
resisted. We should never allow our real mortal bodies to be
used as unholy weapons fighting on the side of sin (cf. Jerusalem
Bible). Quite the contrary, we should always realize that, as
those who with mind and will chose death to sin by entering
into Christ, we are now those who are alive with him by the
power of his resurrection. Thus our bodies are his to use only
for his holy purposes. Once we were slaves of sin. Now we are
God's and servants of obedience unto righteousness.

To put it bluntly: That means conflict! There is no way the
Christian can be neutral. We can be positive, joyous, and creative because we know whose children we are and what he has

called us to. But we also know jolly well where we have come from and what this present scene is all about.

The Wrath of God Versus the Image of the Creator

The same basic assumption underlies the letter to the Colossian Christians (Col. 3). Christians have become sharers in the resurrection life of Christ; therefore their minds are fixed on God and the purpose of God—they see things in ultimate or heavenly terms. And what are the down-to-earth, practical consequences of this? To use gang-land talk, Christians "put out a contract" on all the manifestations of life that are defiling to the image of God's glory in his creation—things like sexual permissiveness or misuse of sex, passions for wrong ends and goals. Marked out especially is that most prominent of the sins of our American culture—coveteousness, materialism, or consumerism. God's wrath is coming down on these kinds of things.

That's not all. The kinds of interpersonal destructiveness that malign and hurt are also part of the evil lifestyle we have to put away. We are to put on, by an act of choice, the new nature which is ours. We are to be like God in our character (Col. 3:10). This means holiness, compassion, kindness, forbearing, forgiving, loving, and much more. We relate to others as God does. This means within the family and in our societal relationships.

Flesh Versus Spirit

How very dynamic is this sense of repentance in every one of Paul's writings! In the Galatian letter he uses the term *flesh* as referring to the whole lifestyle that is alien to the will of God, and the term *Spirit* as that alternative lifestyle that is produced by the Spirit of the living God alive and at work in us. As if we are a bit dense and slow to learn (which we are), he catalogs what *flesh* and *Spirit* look like in the lives they produce. The *flesh* is a bondage that produces destruction. But Christians become, he says, servants of love. Like their Lord Jesus, they give themselves in servitude to others that all may come into the *shalom* of God.

The lifestyle of the flesh is manifested, again, in sexual perversity, false religions and playing with the occult, interpersonal malice, and lack of personal principle and self-control. Conversely, the Holy Spirit in us produces a purposeful, constructive, joyous, ministering, good kind of life that expresses what God is like.

Paul comes back, for a parting shot, just to remind the folks at Galatia that to belong to Christ is to crucify deliberately all self-indulgent passions and desires. In other words, my right-to-myself goes to the cross, gets the axe, and that by my own choice of Jesus Christ!

The Family Likeness of God

I went to visit a family one night in a home where there were several preschool children. The family was quite active in the congregation where I was the pastor. The four-year-old daughter opened the door, looked at me, and yelled over her shoulder: "Hey, Mommie! Jesus is here." I was both amused and sobered. Being the most visible congregational leader had caused me to be identified in her mind with Jesus. But where does a person look in this world to find out what God is like? Take a peek at the letter to the Ephesian Christians (chapter 5). Right in the middle of a very practical discourse on behavior, Paul, almost in passing, says to be imitators of God as his beloved children. Our false and misconstrued humility makes us cringe and shy away from such a word. We tend to shuffle our feet and mumble something about being only sinners saved by grace, as we try to avoid what is said here. Perhaps the reason the world doesn't take us very seriously or find us to be a revolutionary force or a threat to the domain of darkness is because we look and act like everybody else!

In the Hebrew culture the father in a family looked upon his children as his wealth. There wasn't a clear conception of life after death. But the one thing a father did look upon as his life after death was that his children would carry on the family name. He saw generations of sons who would carry on the name, the values, the reputation, and the purposes of the father. Jesus reflects this Hebrew son's concern for his father as he always defers to the name and will of the Father: "Lo, I have come to do thy will." "I and the Father are one." "My Father is working still, and I am working." "He who has seen me has seen the Father." So it should come as no surprise to us that we are called to be like God. If he adopts us into his family by faith in Christ, then the whole watching world has every right to expect us to begin to reflect the family likeness.

Paul will say elsewhere, "Be imitators of me, as I am of Christ" (1 Cor. 11:1). That means that we continually reflect on what God is like and then choose that character, and by the enabling of the Spirit of God we begin to be recreated into that image. Imitators of God!

Sermon on the Mount

The whole Sermon on the Mount (Matt. 5—7) is so alien to everything in the domain of darkness that it makes no sense at all apart from the kingdom of God, the character and will of the Lord God our King. I mean, who could ever get kicks out of being persecuted or mourning or all of that? Just look at the Beatitudes! What a description of happiness or blessedness: the poor in spirit, those who mourn, the meek, those who hunger and thirst for righteousness, the merciful, the pure in heart, the peacemakers, the persecuted and reviled. Uh, uh! That'll never sell.

Only if the blessing of all blessings is God himself does this teaching begin to come into focus. If, as the psalmist says, "In thy presence there is fullness of joy; in thy right hand are pleasures for evermore" (Ps. 16:11), then to belong to God and to be identified with him in his purposes and to be living according to his plan and under his gracious domain makes all kinds of sense. And if that is so, then the Sermon on the Mount makes sense. But it is radical, radical stuff. To be so identified with God through his Son that I can share his heart, mourn over that which grieves him, willingly undergo persecution for him, and share his estimate of who I am will, in fact, bring blessedness.

Holiness is spelled out in substantial passages that jolt us out of our superficial religiosity. Among God's kingdom people, his law is not external but internal and living. The true purpose of the law is effected in our lives so that we reflect life as God intends it. Costly love is the rule of the kingdom. Enemies are loved. True sexuality and God's design in marriage are set forth. Just relations between persons are insisted upon. God's perfection is our own model. The realization of his kingdom is sought; the establishment of his rule and his will on earth becomes our desire and petition.

Look at the economic implications of the kingdom! What happens to banks and insurance companies and stock portfolios if we are not to lay up for ourselves treasure on earth? If our homes and possessions become the sacred treasure of our lives, then we are the possessed and not the possessors. Possessions can be a master, Jesus says. One Christian brother paraphrased this by saying: "Anything I own that I cannot give away owns me."

Simplicity of life and simplicity of trust for bodily needs and apparel are so strange to us. We are captives to fashions and styles—"Give no thought to tomorrow" indeed! But listen to this: To be concerned about what we will eat or drink or wear, Jesus says, puts us in the category of unbelievers (Gentiles).

What is to be first on the minds of kingdom people is God's kingdom and his righteousness. Our care then becomes his concern. How strange that sounds to us. And do you know why it sounds strange? Because we haven't come to grips with the radical nature of the kingdom of God. We are as anxious about tomorrow as any unbeliever, and therefore there is nothing to distinguish us from them.

We are to be very alert to our own needs of cleansing, not trying to find out the wrongs in everybody else. We are to ask God for our needs. We are to recognize that our pathway through this life is a path of discipline, which is not always congenial to the culture. We are to be alert to counterfeits that appear good when they are in fact part of the darkness.

God is to be known. His word is to be done. It is not enough to call him "Lord." It is not enough to do things and call them Christian. God wants to be known by us and to know us. And when he speaks, the purpose of his word is that it be done.

Do you think I'm straying a long way from evangelism? Not at all. We live in a cynical generation when religion is common and religious words clutter the airways. So, what makes this dark world take us seriously? Jesus says that if we live just like everybody else, then we are like saltless salt that has no value at all. If those who profess to be the people of the kingdom of God live out their lives according to the same values and thought patterns as those of the dominion of darkness, then they are not only saltless salt, but are those whose profession, "Lord, Lord," is meaningless. But, Jesus says, when the light is set out there where it illumines the darkness, where it shows what God is like and what his purpose is, where the will of God is fleshed out in human lives for everybody to see—then, people "will see your good works and give glory to your Father who is in heaven" (Matt. 5:16). Is that evangelism? You'd better believe it!

Let's be a bit more specific. The people of the kingdom today can easily go to sleep and fail to see darkness where it is. For instance, we pray for our nation and seek to be good citizens, but we do not wrap our faith in the American flag. We can participate in government because we recognize it for what it is and are forever trying to implement God's will in the affairs of men. But we know that such a course can, for a politician, be politically disastrous. We are under no illusions about the kingdoms of this world. Our first loyalty is to the kingdom of God, and that very loyalty makes us a revolutionary element. We candidly acknowledge that.

We are participants in an economic system called capitalism. But capitalism is not established by scripture, nor is socialism. Wealth in scripture is only a blessing as it is received from God and used for the common good of people. But wealth can also be one of the most oppressive instruments of unrighteousness imaginable. In the law given to the Jews (Lev. 25) property was redistributed every fifty years to keep people from using their wealth to enslave and oppress others. But what of today? Many giant corporations, cartels in labor and industry, destroy people and manipulate nations in ways that the biblical folk only attributed to pagan empires like Assyria.

Look at the issues of prisons, abortion, environment, racism, abused children, poverty, and militarism. Do the Father's children maintain silence in the face of such? Do the citizens of the kingdom of God turn their backs? Is God indifferent? Is the kingdom of light irrelevant?

In this whole section we are dealing with understanding the joyous news of the kingdom of God, or having our Christian facts straight. A most essential point in thinking like a Christian is having a clear grasp on what the Lord calls us to be. Our calling is to be *holy,* to live in a relationship of integrity with the will and character of him who calls us. We are, in fact, a new race, a new creation, a new humanity. Nothing in this world is a matter of indifference to us. "Hallowed be thy name. Thy kingdom come. Thy will be done on earth as it is in heaven." Our calling is to flesh out, amid the stark realities of this age, what the age to come is all about. And when we do we are going to stir up some opposition—but we're also going to whet some appetites, bring some hope, open some hearts, and be able to announce salvation to those dwelling in darkness.

We have been speaking thus far in individual terms. Now on to the communal, or corporate, expression of the kingdom of God.

CHAPTER 5

The Kingdom Between the Ages: The Church as a Sign

God's holy people, God's unique people, don't exist in the world as solitary units. If we're going to think like New Testament Christians we're going to acknowledge right off that Christians are always spoken of as those related to and responsible to a community of believers. But what has this got to do with evangelism, and what has it got to do with the kingdom of God?

Let's go back and pick up some basic points of this whole discussion. Jesus came declaring that a joyous thing had occurred in his coming. That joyous thing was that the gracious dominion of God had broken in upon us, that the darkness was shattered, that hope had dawned, and that repentance and the forgiveness of sins should now be proclaimed to the nations. People are to be called from the kingdom of Satan into God's kingdom, from the dominion of darkness into the dominion of God's dear Son.

What with all the panaceas being hawked and hustled, how are we to convince a cynical, ear-weary populace that there is anything to the claims of Jesus and of the kingdom of God? What are the signs of the kingdom? Is it only talk? All right! In the last chapter we talked about the sign of holy lives, of those who demonstrate in their daily demeanor the character of the King and who do the will of the King. These are the light that causes the world to look and know that God is doing something unique. The thesis of this chapter is that the church is also such a sign of the age to come. How so?

Again, we have to jettison some baggage that is confusing.

There are so many conceptions and misconceptions of what the church is all about that most of us have a difficult time seeing it clearly. It is almost like the deep sea salvage hunters who happen upon some priceless treasure, only it is so crusted with barnacles that it is almost indistinguishable.

Let's look at a thrilling passage of scripture. In the third chapter of the letter to the Ephesians, Paul is talking about the riches of Christ, about the plan of God, the mystery hidden for ages—and then he says that the plan has to do with the fact that "through the church the manifold wisdom of God might now be made known to the principalities and powers in heavenly places" (Eph. 3:10). The statement is so overpowering that it might catch you cold, and you might well miss the import of it. But it conveys the unmistakable fact that God intends to show the power structures of this age what he is up to in the world by means of the church.

Now, brothers and sisters, that puts the church in a light of significance that we often overlook. The reason for our oversight is not hard to find. We usually think of the church in terms of "wineskins" rather than wine, or in terms of its externals and nonessentials rather than its essence. For instance, we think of the church in terms of denominational organizations (Baptists, Roman Catholics, Pentecostals, or Presbyterians), of buildings (Gothic, Colonial, contemporary, or storefront), of congregational organizations, of budgets and programs and committees. Or possibly we, along with much of the public, conceive of the church in terms of those things the media picks up. Many of them are contradictory of the church, even scandalous, such as church squabbles, arguments over issues, departures from theological foundations, and the moral lapses of well-known Christians.

It is such baggage that we must jettison, or at least put in its proper perspective, if we are to see clearly what is the essence of the church and how it relates to the kingdom of God. A proper understanding of what the church is will be a transforming instrument of renewal within the church.

I Will Build My Church

The word "church" is used by Jesus only a few times in the New Testament records. Primarily it is used in the Caesarea Philippi episode when Jesus is asking his disciples who they perceive him to be. They have suggested that the people are identifying him with Elijah, Jeremiah, or one of the prophets. At that point (Matt. 16:15) he asks them pointedly, "But who do you say that I am?" Peter states that Jesus is "the Christ, the Son of the living God." Any way you look at that statement it is dramatic. To identify a person as the anointed one of God, the long-awaited Messiah, the Son of God, in the Jewish community was to indicate the beginning of a new era. It is at this point that Jesus responds with a promise to build a church against which the powers of death, or the gates of hell, should not prevail. This sets the church in a position over against the powers of death and hell.

"Church" is not a cultic word in the Christian community. It was used commonly by the Greeks. It has the flavor of being an assembly called out or called together for a purpose. Jesus states his sovereign intention of calling a people, an assembly, a congregation, a church to himself as Messiah, or Christ. After that episode Jesus only uses the word twice more, and that in the context of resolving a conflict among themselves (Matt. 18:17). What does this have to do with the kingdom of God? Well now, given Jesus' unmistakable teaching of the kingdom, and given the fact that he here accepts again the Messianic identity, doesn't it seem only natural that any assembly or congregation or church he is going to build is going to be the congregation of people who are his kingdom people?

The excitement of the joyous news of the kingdom of God is that the Old Testament expectations of Messiah, of new covenant, of promises, are now being fulfilled in this person, Jesus. And when he begins speaking of building a people, a congregation, it follows that this people is going to be the people of the Messiah, or of the reign of God through his well-beloved Son. This people then becomes the communal evidence of the reign of God, the community of the kingdom. It is here that we will expect to see the character and the will of the King worked out in its interpersonal and communal form. And if they have been called from the domain of death and hell and into the domain of his new life, then we can anticipate that this new community will come across as distinct and unique.

Jesus, in the Gospel records, never sets forth a theological statement about the nature and mission of the church. What you have to realize in reading the scriptures is that he always speaks to the disciples about their lives *together* as they live together in the presence of a world still in the domain of darkness. They are spoken to as "the church before the watching world," to use a current description. They are the manifestation of Christ's kingly rule. They are a sign. The world will respond to his people as it responds to him. They are promised confrontations and persecutions. As they live out his life they can expect tribulation, but in the midst of it they will also share in his peace. They are the people of the age to come, and therefore no power can ultimately overcome them.

Observe that there is nothing solitary or individualistic about the call into Christ's congregation. His call is to himself and into a life of mutual responsibility and interdependence with each other. He does indeed call his sheep by name, but he calls them into his flock.

The Church Is Not the Kingdom

It would be a mistake to identify the church with the kingdom of God. From what we can discern from the scriptures the kingdom is much, much more than the church. God's kingdom has to do with his plan for the ages, to bring all things together and into harmony with himself. It has to do with the "all things new" which are brought about through his Son. Ultimately the kingdom somehow touches heaven and earth, time and eternity, the world of nature and the world of human beings. The kingdom is the redemptive reign of God in creation, inaugurated in the first advent of Jesus, and to be consummated in his glorious return. But the church is the community of that kingdom and the sign of the kingdom, and that is enough to put some "zing" in our conception of who we are and of our evangelistic calling.

Plan for the Ages

At this point I am very aware of how little we conceive of the church as part of the joyous news. As a matter of fact, there are a lot of congregations that are anything but joyous news. But it is a mistake to lose sight of the fact that the church is part of the new wine of the gospel. We need to take a long draught from the letter to the Ephesians where this marvel is spelled out so eloquently.

First off, you will want to keep in mind that this letter is written to the church, so that it is addressed to *you* in the plural, and speaks of *us* and of *we*. I say this only by way of reminder that it is not addressed to a bunch of solitary individuals, but to persons dwelling together in assemblies or congregations who minister to one another, who are responsible to and for one another. And they are *holies*, or saints (verse 1). They are living in a relationship of harmony with the character and will of God. That makes them unique in the world, even peculiar. That makes them a sign, as we discussed in the last chapter.

Notice (chapter 1) now how Paul develops this theme of the "plan for the fulness of time" or the "plan of the mystery hidden for ages" (3:9). He rejoices right off that we have been *blessed* with every spiritual blessing in the "realm of the real" by Jesus Christ. He confirms the fact that God has *chosen* us to be a people who are both holy and blameless and full of love. In the most extravagant terms he exults in our redemption, our forgiveness, the riches of grace lavished upon us in Jesus Christ. But this all leads up to the fact that God has unfolded to us and given us the wisdom and insight to comprehend his plan, his master plan. And that master plan is to bring everything back together again into harmony with himself. It is the plan to unite all things in Christ, things in heaven and on earth.

In the accomplishing of this plan the gospel is preached, and persons believe that joyous news and are sealed or stamped with the seal of the Holy Spirit. That Spirit is the same Spirit that raised up Jesus from the dead; so there is immeasurable power at work in the church as Jesus dynamically and progressively manifests his Lordship over all things.

God, who accomplishes whatsoever he wills, has called us from death to life. We have been called (chapter 2) out of the domain of death, where we were captives to the immediate desires of our mere humanity. But we need to see that it is not only a deliverance *from* the malignant dominion of Satan, but it is a redemption that translates us into a people who share in all that belongs to Christ, so that the Father might manifest in us his boundless grace and kindness. Moreover, we are created a whole new breed of humanity that we might flesh out the character and will of God, that is, walk in good works.

One of the major evidences of this plan and of this new breed of humanity is the fact that within the new humanity all the dividing walls that separate are broken down. Traditional walls, prejudice, classes, clan hostility, and the like are all broken down; hostility comes to an end, and all of us become one new family in Christ, and all have equal access to the Father by the same Holy Spirit. This new family, or new humanity, then becomes God's dwelling place by the Holy Spirit (2:21–22). Choruses of "Praise God!" ought to be welling up in our hearts by now.

Brothers and sisters, can you begin to handle the fact that the church is where God lives—is his dwelling place by the Holy Spirit—so that when people in this present darkness are looking for God—who he is and what he is like—they have every right to look at the church for the answers?

In the cultural setting of this first-century letter the major barrier seemed to be the one between Jews and Gentiles. Translate that into twentieth-century language and it might come out that we need to expect God to draw unto himself the most unlikely peoples, the most irreligious and despised. It is this very working of God's power in creating a new and unique community where walls of prejudice are broken down that is a witness to the power structures of this world, the principalities and powers (3:10). Digest that fact! Through the church God witnesses to the reality of his kingly and redemptive purpose, and the objects of that witness are the power structures of the dominion of darkness.

Because this is so very glorious, Paul again and again breaks out into joyous expressions of praise and prayer that we might all recognize and enter more fully into the experience of God's immeasurable love and power. Now, fasten your seat belts! Look very thoughtfully at this:

> Now to him who by the power at work within us is able to do far more abundantly than all that we ask or think, to him be glory in the church and in Christ Jesus to all generations, for ever and ever. Amen.
>
> (Eph. 3:20–21)

Glory in the church and in Christ Jesus! Can you accept the fact that God chooses to demonstrate, or to express his redemptive purpose, in the assembly of his people, in the new humanity, just as he does in his Son? And lest that overwhelm you, note that in this ascription of praise, Paul states that this is accomplished by the power at work in us; and this power is able to do far more than we can even imagine. This is that power, earlier mentioned, which raised Jesus Christ from the dead, namely the Holy Spirit.

The calling of the church, then, is not to be some effete religious gathering, but to be the very authentication of the plan of God in Christ Jesus. It is a new community in which God dwells by his Spirit to show to all this darkened age his own glory, his own character and redemptive will. By its very being, as it is true to its calling, the church is a sign of the age to come, and is therefore evangelistic. It is only as it fades into the landscape of darkness and becomes merely a religious expression of the darkness that it ceases to be evangelistic. When the inner life of the community contradicts the character and will of God, then the church becomes part of the darkness. When walls of prejudice and lovelessness go back up and when forgiveness and grace are replaced by sectarian and prideful judgmentalism, then the church ceases to manifest the plan of God.

The remainder of the Ephesian letter spells out in practical detail what the church looks like in real day-by-day terms:

1) It is a community where our calling to be God's people is visibly demonstrated in love, in mutual lowliness, meekness, patience, forbearance, and peaceable unity (4:1–4). The classic work on the Christian community in these terms is *Life Together,* by Dietrich Bonhoeffer.

2) It is a community of charismatic gifts given by the ascended Lord so that every member becomes part of the ministry and in a unique fashion contributes to the building up of the whole into the likeness of the head of the body, who is Christ (4:7–16).

3) It is a community that eschews the behavior patterns that are part of the Gentile (unbelieving) culture and that violate the character of God and his purpose for his creation. It becomes, thereby, a community that is like God in true righteousness and holiness (4:17–24).

4) It is a community of brotherly love and caring, where all that hurts and deceives and exploits is deliberately put away, and where the edifying and forgiving kindness of God is expressed in all relationships, so as to exhibit the family likeness of the Father (4:25—5:2).

5) It is the community of the kingdom of Christ and of God (5:5), where all the gross expressions of darkness have no place. Named are such expressions as empty talk, sexual looseness, obsessions with possessions, dirtiness, and whatever else is part of the unfruitful works of darkness. The reason behind this is that we used to be part of the darkness, but now we are light in the Lord and are thereby to walk as children of light (5:8).

6) It is a community of worship. In this new community praise, thanksgiving, singing, rejoicing, mutual encouragement, and instruction in the will of God are the flavor of times together. There is to be that life-giving working of the Holy Spirit that is so lively that it is almost intoxicating (5:15–20).

7) It is a community of redemptive relationships in fami-

lies, between husbands and wives, between parents and children. Redemptive relationships also are expressed to those outside the new community, in the relationships between employers and employees—slaves and masters (5:21—6:9).

8) It is a community involved in the cosmic conflict between the darkness and light. The church is promised that a continual spiritual warfare will be its lot but that by standing full in its heritage in Christ it will prevail (6:10–20).

Isn't that mind-boggling? What a view of the church as part of the new wine of the gospel! Into a world of lonely, fractured, hopeless people God comes creating a new people who express his caring, purposeful character and are in actuality his own family where his intention toward his own is fleshed out in day-by-day practicality.

Powers of the Age to Come

Since the church is this kind of dwelling place of God by the Spirit, anyone who participates in this new community will experience, in part, the life of the age to come. The Holy Spirit being present in the congregation of God's people, there will be those kinds of joy, praise, love, and even healings and marvelous answers to prayer that are humanly unexplainable. Such is only to be expected if the church is in fact the community of the kingdom of God, if it is in fact the congregation or assembly of the age to come dwelling in this present age. It follows that the ordinary congregational life of God's people is also very evangelistic, as the new wine of the gospel is experienced in our mutual lives.

In a troublesome passage in the letter to the Hebrew Christians, the writer speaks of those, evidently by virtue of their participation in the community, who have once been enlightened, who have tasted the heavenly gift, and have become partakers of the Holy Spirit, and have tasted the goodness of the word of God and the powers of the age to come . . ." (Heb. 6:4–5). He is speaking concerning those who having had this experience in the community then turn against Christ and commit "apostasy." But the passage is very enlightening in terms of showing us what the community of God's people is to be like. If we can lift this passage out of its context having to do with apostasy, and look at what even a person off the streets should be experiencing as he or she becomes involved in the assembly, it clues us in to the evangelistic character of the community, which is the community of the age to come, or of the kingdom of God. It is alive. It is enlightening. The gifts of the Holy Spirit and the Holy Spirit himself are literally experienced. The word of God is present. There is a humanly unexplainable power at work in the saints, both in their transformed lives and in the marvelous works and signs that accompany the gospel. The church is in actuality "holy ground."

As the World Looks On

It is fascinating to look at the letters of the New Testament, those letters written to the church, and to see what is the flavor of the church. To pursue this topic would cause this chapter to expand into a volume or more. But the world looking on has a right to expect some things to be true of the church. In the inner life of the congregation and in the mutual ministry of members to each other the world has a right to see what God's family is like, what the body of Christ is all about. There should be those evidences that have always been referred to as the *marks* of the church: witness, worship, fellowship, and service. Onlookers should see resurrection hope and joy, a concern for truth, for persons, and for the future. Most of all, they should see us loving each other as Christ loved us (John 13:34–35). By this they are to know that we are his disciples.

But outwardly they also have a right to look on and see some of the concerns that are expressive of the character and will of God. They should see the church members as careful custodians and stewards of God's creation, of environment, of natural resources. After all, "this is my Father's world"! They should expect to see the Father's zeal for righteousness and justice

expressed in the intensity of our zeal for justice and righteousness. And they should expect to see the Father's compassion for
the poor, the oppressed, the hungry, the naked, the imprisoned,
the orphans and widows fleshed out in those compassionate
lives that bring more than empty words. The congregation of
Christ's people should be the friend of sinners. Incarnating
itself in the darkness, it should be bringing light and help and
hope to the lost world that Christ came to seek and to save.

Wineskins

At this point, if you are a thinking person, you are going to
be in the process of computing all of this biblical data and then
looking at the particular çongregation that you are most familiar with and asking the question: "Can he be talking about my
congregation?" The disparity between some of these biblical
patterns and our experience of the church can sometimes be a
bit disconcerting. The First Church of River City can look nothing at all like the church in Ephesus.

We do need to disenchant ourselves with the notion that the
New Testament churches were all churches in a state of revival
and unblemished fullness of the Holy Spirit. Not so! The church
is always the church between the ages. It is always made up of
wheat and tares sown together. There is always some admixture
of darkness and light. Because of this there is perennially the
emergence of strife, of error, of sterility, of compromise, of
schism, in short, of darkness within the church.

This tension is nowhere more graphically seen than in the
letters to the seven churches in Revelation, chapters 2 and 3.
Here were congregations in Asia Minor, all of which had valid
beginnings. Yet within a few years only two of them are com-
mended without reservation. The others were in spiritual dan-
ger and were warned that unless they repented and got back
to their calling they might well cease to be churches, and their
lamps would be removed from the lampstand. Their light was
almost darkness. And this happens. A congregation true to its
calling in one generation vanishes in the next, or becomes a

memorial society for a church that was once a lively community but is now only a building.

The church is of the essence of the new wine of the gospel. It is forever. It is the community of the kingdom that is God's work. Yet somehow, in the mystery of God's working, it exists in wineskins that are not of the essence of the wine, but, rather, are human forms that change from one place to another and from one generation to another. These wineskins are the institutional forms of the church: the First Baptist Church on the corner, the Benedictine monastery at Subiaco, the Diocese of the Episcopal Church, or the believers meeting in a house church in secret in a Chinese village. Somehow the believers meeting and living out their lives together are of the wine, they are the assembly which Jesus Christ is building and which the gates of hell shall not prevail against. But the house, the structure, the organization, the building are wineskins and, while useful to contain and convey the wine in one period, may become too rigid and useless in another place or time.

The wineskin problem becomes apparent particularly in missions when we try to transfer a wineskin that is useful in one culture to another culture where it is a hindrance. And yet God continues to call persons into community, into his "age-to-come people," in vastly differing locales, cultures, and historical settings.

It becomes our task as those who are members of the body, and who are the church, always to be aware of who we are. As members of the local assembly, or congregation, we need periodically to look at the wineskin in which we live and ask questions about its capacity to convey dynamically the new wine of the gospel. Are we expressive of the new covenant? of the kingdom of God? Are we aware of why God has called us to himself? Have we become tamed and enculturated to the point that we are indistinguishable from the other institutions of darkness? Can people discern the salvation of God in our corporate life? Are we a friend of sinners?

You see, the kingdom community, the church, is a necessity in evangelism because it is that community in which the gospel is authenticated. It is here that God's plan to bring all things together in himself is seen in the midst of fractured humanity. It is here that the world may look at our claims of joyous news, and know that our beliefs work themselves out in a whole new breed of humanity, in God's new covenant humanity. The New Testament never conceives of evangelism apart from this new community which is the church.

This being so, it is incumbent upon us continually to evaluate and reevaluate our buildings, budgets, organizations, programs, denominations, ecumenical structures, traditions, and procedures with much prayer and searching of scriptures to discern their usefulness in the plan of God for his church. Because all of these things are wineskins. And our concern in evangelism is that the joyous news of the kingdom of God be manifest in the kingdom community.

Summary

To this point we have been briefly looking at that New Testament *understanding* of the joyous news of Jesus Christ that enables us to think like Christians, having our facts straight. We looked at the nature of the dominion of darkness, which is the alien force that rules this age. Then we looked at the joyous news of the kingdom of God, which was inaugurated in the birth, life, death, and resurrection of Jesus Christ. We saw that this kingdom is now dynamically present, yet is not consummated until the second advent of Jesus Christ. At that point the kingdoms of this world will become the kingdoms of our God and of his Christ.

Finally, we looked at two authenticating evidences of the kingdom of God in this "between the ages" period, evidences which are critical to our evangelistic task: holy lives and a holy church. Now we must pass on to the *experiencing* of the joyous news of the kingdom: Are we experiencing a living relationship to God through Jesus Christ? Are we part of his kingdom? Are we intoxicated with the new wine of the gospel?

SECTION II
Experiencing the Joyous News of the Kingdom of God

Something which has existed since the beginning,
that we have heard,
and we have seen with our own eyes;
that we have watched
and touched with our hands:
the Word, who is life—
this is our subject.
That life was made visible:
we saw it and we are giving our testimony,
telling you of the eternal life
which was with the Father and has been made visible to us.
What we have seen and heard
we are telling you
so that you too may be in union with us,
as we are in union
with the Father
and with his Son Jesus Christ.
We are writing this to you to make our own joy complete.

(1 John 1:1–4, Jerusalem Bible)

CHAPTER 6
The Care and Feeding
of the Evangelists

"O.K., 'Rev,' dat sounds super. How d'ya get plugged in?"
That was the question put to me by a teenager from an inner-
city neighborhood at a summer Bible camp. I had been explain-
ing the Christian faith to a group of high school students for
about a week when he came forth with his very pointed question, "How d'ya get plugged in?" That is the subject before us
in this second section, as we move from the data of the gospel
of the kingdom in the first section to the evangelistic task in the
third section.

To know the gospel of the kingdom is one thing, but to be
so joyously related to the Lord our Savior that we spontaneously
express that new life of his kingdom people is something else.
How do we grow into maturity? How do we appropriate the
new life that is promised us in the New Testament? What are
we to expect as the experience of the gospel? There is no little
mystery here. The diversity of Christian experience forbids that
we fall into any neat formulas on "sure-fire methods of spiritual
growth." So, also, is one modest about dogmatizing that "this is
the way to become a Christian."

Martin Luther rested in the fact of his baptism: "I have been
baptized!" In his mind he became a Christian at that point, even
though it all became real to him in solitary Bible study. Eldridge
Cleaver professes to have had a vision, a mystical experience,
while in political exile. William Orange, a New Zealand Anglican pastor, was converted by hearing the liturgy as a youth

while singing in the choir. Some grow up from childhood with a firm faith in Jesus Christ. Others go through dramatic experiences. John Wesley was an ordained and practicing missionary and pastor long before that heart-warming experience in the Aldersgate Meeting House in London at which point he was "converted."

Can one believe and yet not be converted? Can one know all the data of the New Testament faith and accept it as true and yet not be evangelized? I believe so! Theologically that may be a troublesome answer. Yet it is demonstrated over and over again, as in Wesley's case. Was Wesley a believer before Aldersgate? Well, I'm quite willing to leave that to God. I'm willing to believe that he was a Christian, though with all kinds of misapprehensions about his soul, with doubts, and without any gospel joy. At Aldersgate it became real. At that point he became convinced, converted, and contagious.

But why use a super-figure like Wesley? The same thing has happened to many persons we all know. Somebody is a respected church member, quotes the Apostles' Creed with integrity, and yet is joyless, cautious, restrained, doubtful about many aspects of his or her own Christian experience. Then, at some moment, through some circumstances that you have to assign to the gracious Lord, there is an experience when the lights go on, the shadows are dispelled, the doubts vanish, love and joy and peace and excitement begin to overflow—and that person is evangelized! Praise God!

Such an evangelizing moment is not the exception in the New Testament. It is normative. It is mysterious. It is the working of the Spirit of God. And it is obvious that the Lord wants his people to be convinced, converted, and contagious. Paul tells the Roman Christians that he wants to come and evangelize them (Rom. 1:15). He wants to remind them and excite them afresh with the joyous news of Jesus and the kingdom.

In other places Paul records his prayers for congregations that they may experience in an ever new and increasing way the reality of the gospel.

> I do not cease to give thanks for you, remembering you
> in my prayers, that the God of our Lord Jesus Christ, the
> Father of glory, may give you a spirit of wisdom and of
> revelation in the knowledge of him, having the eyes of
> your hearts enlightened, that you may know what is the
> hope to which he has called you, what are the riches of
> his glorious inheritance in the saints, and what is the
> immeasurable greatness of his power in us who believe,
> according to the working of his great might which he
> accomplished in Christ when he raised him from the
> dead. . . .   (Eph. 1:16–20a)

John writes to Christian people in his first letter, so that they may have an assured knowledge that they have eternal life. Jesus promises his disciples peace in the midst of tribulation, and joy in their walk with him as disciples. The Christian life in the early church appears to be a life that is marked by joy and praise and boldness in the midst of the most difficult circumstances. In the New Testament writings there is nothing of the pious but joyless agnosticism that we experience so often in the church today. Neither was unevangelized orthodoxy set forth as a norm. It may be about such sterile zeal for orthodoxy that Jesus spoke when he told the church at Ephesus that they had abandoned the love they had at first (see Rev. 2:4).

It is interesting to learn in recent mission studies that most of the persons who engage in one-on-one evangelistic conversations are persons who have been Christians for a relatively short time. Why so? Because they are still excited by the gospel. Their faith is fresh and alive and contagious. They have experienced the truth and they know how liberating it is and they cannot wait for an occasion to share it with someone else. They also remember from what they have been delivered and have some compassion on those who are still in darkness.

Are there, then, disciplines by which we can enter more profoundly into the new life in Christ? Are there practices by which we can be evangelized and reevangelized so that we become, individually and corporately, instruments of the joyous news, to make it known spontaneously and joyously to persons and societies that dwell yet in the darkness? Yes there are! And this is the issue before us now. Before we can be evangelizers we must be thoroughly evangelized, individually and as congregations. Only then can we be effective instruments in God's hand to herald the joyous news of Jesus Christ, of the kingdom of God, of eternal life, of forgiveness, of grace and truth and hope. So let's set ourselves to this task and let's start at the beginning, with the first steps.

The Congregation as Evangelist

There are three words that are used in the New Testament to describe the action one takes in responding to the preaching of the gospel of the kingdom, the joyous news of Jesus Christ. They are: *repent, believe,* and be *baptized.* These are the prominent ones. I want to stress the third one for a moment because it was the public rite of entering into the new community of faith. It was expressive of repentance and faith, but it was also the public entrance rite into the church. To be baptized into Christ was to be identified with his body, the church. I say this because in our evangelical tradition in more recent years we have spoken of Christian faith and growth with the emphasis on the personal experience, leaving unspoken the necessity of the congregation.

Frankly, I have not seen much wholesome Christian growth, or spiritual formation, done by solitary Christians. So I want to speak of some biblical disciplines and expectations having to do with spiritual formation, and I want to speak of them both in the sense of personal disciplines and of corporate disciplines. These are both essential dimensions to Christian growth.

Spiritual formation in isolation from the Christian community tends to be plastic and unreal. Conversely, spiritual formation only in the Christian community, where the individual believers have not spent time alone with God, can be dilute and superficial.

So let's encourage a healthy balance. If spiritual formation has to do with the care and feeding of the evangelists, then we must acknowledge that there is a good deal of kingdom reality that is "caught and not taught." The congregation is also an evangelist, and the disciplines of its corporate life in Christ convey, in a powerful way, the reality of the joyful news of the kingdom of God.

I don't want to belabor this point wearisomely, but just as an individual person may be a believer and yet not be converted or evangelized, so it is increasingly apparent to me that a congregation may have the same problem. It may, as a congregation, have all the components of a true church, and yet be sterile, a religious club that conveys anything but the joyous news of the kingdom. So, in talking about the disciplines of spiritual formation, we automatically fall over into what is called "church renewal."

In my own experience this has been graphically demonstrated. I became the pastor of a congregation that had the kind of internal strife that made me the fourth pastor in a five year period. There were regular services, duly ordained elders and deacons, weekly prayer meetings, and all of that; but the members were, for the most part, anxious, joyless, and unloving. Naturally the congregation was decreasing in size. One member put it baldly: "I don't know why anyone would ever want to belong to this church—I don't want to belong to it myself!" Evidently and obviously there could be no interest in or capacity for evangelism in such a context.

Yet over the next several years, as scriptures were taught and the Spirit of God moved upon lives, there was a most notable change, and not only in individuals. This estranged bunch of individuals became a true family of Christians who cared for each other and were expressing their joyous faith in areas of human need outside the congregation. One day, about six years after the above episode, a lady walked into my office and said: "I want to talk to you. I have been a member of another congregation all of my life, but something is going on here. I have visited several times and it is obvious that your people not only believe something, but they really love each other. Tell me what is going on. I've never seen this in a congregation."

Now there's evangelism! When a church is evangelized, it

naturally becomes an evangelist. And this is why the evangelizing of the congregation is of necessity a critical part of spiritual
formation.

The Form of the Christian Community

I'm using the term *Christian community* to speak of that
gathering of believers in which spiritual formation takes place.
You could speak of a church, a congregation, an assembly, a
small group, or whatever. All I want you to grasp is the concept
of a group of believers who are incorporate in Christ.

The question, though, will immediately be raised: What is
the form of the Christian community in which spiritual formation effectively takes place? Is it a large congregation of several
hundred or several thousand members replete with paid clergy
and all the ecclesiastical accouterments? Or is it a small group
of half-a-dozen or a dozen folks meeting in someone's home for
Bible study and sharing?

This is a critical question. We are at a point in history when
questions rightly are being raised about large institutional
churches. The "Jesus Revolution," that enormous revival that
took place within the youth culture in the late sixties and early
seventies, spun off thousands of small and effective house
churches. It also produced some free-form congregations that
have thousands of members. This is not a new phenomenon.
Many church historians have related the effectiveness of the
Wesleyan revival to Wesley's "class meetings" where small
numbers of believers accepted responsibility for each other. At
the same time, we ordinarily think of the church in terms of a
large group of believers meeting together on Sunday morning.
So the question is proper: In what form does spiritual formation
take place most effectively?

And the answer is probably that, ideally, both are necessary.
There are things that larger congregations can do more effectively. There is something good and exciting about celebrative
worship in a large company of believers. There are areas of

service and missionary outreach that are accomplished more effectively through a large group with the assets available to them.

I would venture to say at this point, however, that a large congregation ought to be composed of a cluster of small fellowship groups, or house churches, where people are known, accepted, cared for, and where true interdependence can be expressed as it cannot be in large congregations. I would propose that these fellowship groups should be rallied around an elder who is a mature Christian and to whom the group willingly submits in leadership. The larger congregation, then, would be under a session or council of elders composed of these leaders of house-church fellowship groups. The task of this council of elders would be to give oversight and direction to the larger congregation. That would make the elders what they are supposed to be, models of faith and shepherds of the flock who keep careful oversight of the Lord's sheep. There is substantial New Testament evidence for such a structure.

The New Testament seems to view the Christian community in the form of house churches that are small enough for individuals to know and be known and where the gift that each member has is called forth and expressed in mutual ministry. In such a setting elders can keep oversight with integrity and give answer to the Lord (Heb. 13:17) for those committed to their charge. And yet these house churches in a community obviously met together and were in some kind of connectional relation to each other, so that the apostle could address a letter to the church at Philippi and know that it would be read to the body of Christ in that city.

I am willing to pursue this point, because a believer may join a large congregation, and yet be very lonely and virtually isolated from any caring fellowship in that large company of believers. At the same time, if a believer is assigned to, or becomes part of, a house-church fellowship group where there is mutual caring and commitment, it is impossible to get lost and be lonely. The kind of disciplines that follow here presuppose the kind of intimate fellowship that is provided in smaller units such as a house church. But they do not denigrate the excitement of the larger congregation and the place it has in worship, the sacraments, and the encouragement of the believer.

CHAPTER 7
Honest Inquiry
and a Community of Truth

A brief statement needs to be made here about the wholesomeness of honest inquiry into the data of the Christian faith. A practice that often leads to spiritual disaster is that of hustling persons into Christian profession or church membership before they ever have an opportunity to look carefully at the facts of the faith or the cost of Christian discipleship. In our sales-oriented society we want to make the sale and get the name on the dotted line as quickly as possible.

Granted, there are some persons who are convinced of Jesus Christ on the basis of a very simple statement and a minimum of knowledge. They are ready to give him their lives because, in their own personal spiritual bankruptcy, they see no other way. An English pastor tells the story of walking into a large cathedral one day out of curiosity to test the acoustics. He, in full pulpit voice, spoke the words of John the Baptist: "Behold the Lamb of God who taketh away the sins of the world!" And then, satisfied, he left. A short time later there was a knock at his office door and a man entered. The man had been an artisan working high up in the dome of that cathedral and had heard the words, had come under conviction of his need spiritually, and had sought out the person who spoke the word. Upon the basis of a simple statement he had come under conviction. After a brief explanation he had come to faith in Christ.

But for others it is not so simple. The more our culture moves into a very secular humanism, the more the whole notion of any "god" becomes remote in the minds of large portions of the society. And the more we are deluged with cults and oriental religions with all their mystical experiences, the more the darkness becomes pathological in persons' minds. This means that the Christian community needs to encourage thoughtful inquiry and honest questioning on the part of those for whom we are concerned.

The Christian community must not be defensive. It is not as though the Christian faith were fragile. Our faith is built upon objective revelation. God has made himself known. Jesus Christ has come with a candid claim that whoever has seen him has seen the Father. The church is called, among other things, "the pillar and bulwark of the truth" (1 Tim. 3:15). A person who is persuaded to make profession while still harboring serious reservations or doubts or misunderstandings will always be unhealthy until those questions are resolved.

Many persons who have grown up in the context of, let me say it kindly, "diseased" Christian congregations have all kinds of emotional reservations about the validity of what they hear. What they see in the scriptures is at such variance with what they have experienced. They need some context in which to air this contradiction.

There needs to be a place for inquirers in Bible study groups. There need to be evangelistic or inquirers' Bible studies where the data of the scriptures is looked at, discussed, and where its claims are faced. Jesus Christ is either who he says he is, or he isn't. He is either true or he is a deceiver. A person needs to have a context in which to look carefully at the data about Jesus Christ, the claims of Jesus Christ, and the demands of Jesus Christ.

It is often the questions or challenges of such inquirers that put the finger on some of the pretense and sterility of the Christian community. This also is healthy. I personally have learned more about myself, the church, and theology from such artless and brash young inquirers than I have anywhere else.

There are risks to such a discipline of inquiry, especially for the Christian community. Intellectual questions arise. Behavioral questions arise. Ethical questions arise. Yet this is enormously healthy. It brings out into the light questions that need to be faced, and our Christian faith and community give us a healthy context in which to face them.

The Christian community must be patient with inquirers. Even though there is an urgency in the Christian message, there is also the fact that some persons need time to listen, ponder, sort out, think through all of the tangled and confused thoughts that they come with in the light of the unique and all-encompassing claims of Jesus Christ. We can trust the Holy Spirit to bring forth joyous faith when a person understands the truth. There is a ministry of sowing and watering the seed that precedes the increase that God gives.

The kingdom of God is so absolutely contrary to the dominion of darkness that we need to expect people to listen, to shake their heads with incredulity, to blink their eyes in amazement, and frequently to go off to a quiet place to figure out if these things can be true. We need, then, to allow a generous place for genuine inquiry at the threshold of spiritual formation.

CHAPTER 8
The Discipline of Repentance in a Community of Repentance

Whatever our profession of Christian faith may be, if we are still wedded to the thought patterns and value systems of the dominion of darkness we're going to be saltless salt, the empty "Lord, Lord" mouthers that Jesus professes not to know (Matt. 7:21–23).

This is why *repentance* always stands at the threshold of belief in the preaching of the New Testament.

> "The time is fulfilled, and the kingdom of God is at hand; repent, and believe in the gospel." (Mark 1:15)

> And Peter said to them, "Repent, and be baptized every one of you in the name of Jesus Christ for the forgiveness of your sins; and you shall receive the gift of the Holy Spirit." (Acts 2:38)

Repentance just may be the forgotten discipline of the Christian and the Christian community. There are very few churches that call forth a deliberate sense of repentance in inviting persons into the community of faith. And this may explain the often effete character of our corporate and personal testimony.

As one example, in a recent missionary consultation it seemed fitting to this particular body to speak to the testimony of our use or misuse of wealth. There came a call for a "new economic order" that would seek to remedy the huge disparity between the wealthy nations of the world and the struggling, poverty-stricken nations of the Third World. The call recognized the fact that the wealthy nations and the multi-national corporations which are part of these nations are looked upon by the poorer nations as oppressors.

Now, on the face of it, biblically, the call was easily justifiable. But because we have often fawned over wealthy persons (by biblical standards most of us middle-class people are "wealthy") in the church, and welcomed them into the Christian community with all of their reverence for capitalism, and never once whispered that the kingdom of God puts a whole new face on the possession and use of wealth—because of this lack of repentance or call for repentance, the missionary consultation call hit the fan with a violence that was startling. Charges of "socialism" and other pejorative comments were instantly forthcoming from members of the church.

The Bible certainly doesn't condemn the possession of wealth. But it does have a very great deal to say about its use.

> But if any one has the world's goods and sees his brother in need, yet closes his heart against him, how does God's love abide in him? Little children, let us not love in word or speech but in deed and in truth.
> (1 John 3:17–18)

This is one small passage, but it is representative of a very large stream of teaching about the use of wealth and the concern for the poor that runs through the whole of scripture. Wealthy people don't come off too easily in scripture. So the Christian community has some obligation to say to those who seek entrance into the community of the kingdom of God: "Mr. Prosperous, in the name of Jesus we want to welcome you into the community which is his. We need to say very clearly, however, that you are a person of considerable wealth and influence, and that this is, on the one hand, possibly perilous to you spiritually. On the other hand, your wealth must now be available to the King, because it all belongs to him. As long as there are hungry and helpless people in the world, we as the King's people have a responsibility. This has economic consequences. Do you still want to be part of his people?"

That puts practical repentance right out there where it belongs. Another kind of example is that of a young man who was part of the youth culture of the sixties, who said to me: "Bob, I'd like to give my life to Jesus, but I've been sleeping with my chick for three years now. Would I have to give that up? It's a hard habit to break!" Repentance would insist that such a relationship either be formalized in the institution of marriage, or broken off. But it cannot welcome into the Father's family those who would exploit sex carelessly.

We need to keep clearly in mind that the whole dominion of darkness with its values, lifestyles, philosophies, mistaken loyalties, and defiling effects is opposed to and at warfare with the dominion of our Lord Jesus Christ. They are competing loyalties. "You cannot worship God and mammon." "Do not walk in the flesh, but walk in the Spirit." "Turn from darkness to light and from the power of Satan unto God." "You were slaves of sin, but now you are servants of righteousness." "You were lost but now are found." These biblical injunctions show clearly how mutually exclusive are these two dominions and how clear is the call for repentance.

Jesus taught that one thing the Holy Spirit would do when he came would be to "show where wrong and right and judgement lie" (John 16:8, NEB). The Holy Spirit makes the issue with the world. He distinguishes between sin and righteousness and makes the consequences plain. It is unthinkable then to consider talking about participating in Christ and in the kingdom of God unless our loyalties are with him, unless his own holy character and will become the standard for our holy lives and behavior.

The word *repentance* is from a Greek word having to do with a change or transformation of mind. It speaks to a reorientation of thinking and values. In this "present age" or dominion of darkness we have a confused and distorted picture of what is going on. But the Eternal Sovereign comes among us in his glory, and we have the truth before us, and we are called upon to get our hearts and minds into harmony with him. Then, and only then, are we promised all the blessings of forgiveness and new life in him. Here at the beginning a moral choice has to be made.

Repentance Unto Life

About the word *repentance* hangs the connotation of something that is a gloomy necessity in order to attain eternal life. This probably betrays our affinity for the darkness, or a rather dismal view of eternal life. Repentance is *unto life.* Repentance is because the darkness has been exposed by the light of the gospel. Repentance is unto the light and into the joyous kingdom of light. There is nothing gloomy or dismal about it. Repentance is a discovery. It is a discovery that "sin pays a wage, and the wage is death, but God gives freely, and his gift is eternal life, in union with Christ Jesus our Lord" (Rom. 6:23, NEB).

The Christian person and the Christian community are those who are alert to the tragedy of this present age. While on the one hand a Christian always desires to affirm what is good and beautiful and creative and just in the culture, at the same time Christians are children of the light who expose the unfruitful works of darkness.

But it is not a groveling in the darkness that characterizes the children of light. We are not to be like the "muck-rakers" of journalistic notoriety who delight in digging up dirt. No! We are to be those who delight in the Lord. We are those who, having been called into the light, are now discovering what abundant life is all about. We are looking for ways to express the great *shalom* of God in the midst of this very real and tragic present age. This may be nowhere better expressed than in the prayer of St. Francis:

> Lord, make me an instrument of your peace.
> Where there is hatred, let me sow love.
> Where there is injury, pardon.
> Where there is doubt, faith.
> Where there is despair, hope.
> Where there is darkness, light.
> Where there is sadness, joy.

O Divine Master, grant that I may not so much seek
To be consoled as to console,
To be understood as to understand,
To be loved as to love,
For it is in giving that we receive;
It is in pardoning that we are pardoned;
It is in dying that we are born to eternal life.

True repentance will be culture creating. It will be always
dynamic in seeking to express the will of God "on earth as in
heaven." We, by an act of will, do make an initial judgment
about darkness and light and so repent at the entrance to our
Christian lives. But repentance is also that life-long discipline of
discerning between darkness and light and joyfully responding
to the light.

Repentance is costly. The account of Jesus and the rich
young man has deep significance. Jesus loved him very much,
the scripture records. But Jesus discerned in him a tie to another loyalty, namely his wealth. Again, this is no condemnation
of wealth—unless that wealth is an idol. And so it was for the
young man. Jesus issued a moral challenge to the young man to
divest himself of his wealth, give it to the poor, and then take
up a life of discipleship. The light exposed the darkness and the
young man, for all of his fine traits, chose the darkness and went
away sorrowing.

We need the encouragement and the refining ministry of
the Christian community in a life and discipline of repentance.
Our motives are so mixed. We share so much moral confusion
with the culture around us. More than we know, we are conformed to the world, brainwashed by the media, and sometimes
led astray by mistaken spirits within the church. But, more
normally, the congregation of Christian persons serves to support us in living as children of light. The mutual encouragement
and supportive exhortations give us strength. The discussions,
preaching, and fellowship of the Christian community assist in
clarifying issues and sorting out conflicting claims. The Holy
Spirit enlightens and strengthens us corporately so that we may
know and do the will of our Heavenly Father. We need this

community in the Holy Spirit as the clash of loyalties becomes more complex in an increasingly secular and humanistic "global village," where not just personal choices are involved, but choices that affect people halfway around the earth.

To read the challenge in the sixth chapter of Romans at one level is to realize that a baptized person, being now one with Christ in his death to sin and resurrection unto new life, can have no truck with a sinful lifestyle. That principle is unimpeachable. We read also that we have forsaken slavery in unrighteousness unto sin for willing devotion and service in righteousness unto Christ. Okay. But when you begin to translate that into—

Personal loyalties
Personal habits
Political convictions
Economic choices
Responsibility to the poor and helpless
Business,, medical, and professional ethics
Traditions
Lifestyles ("Live simply that others may simply live!")
Goals
Family life
Civic affairs
Awareness of unrighteousness in the culture

—then, you see, you are dealing in areas where black and white do not always appear in quite such clear contrast. That does not mean that we become pessimists or cynics. But it is in such areas that "thy will be done on earth" becomes visible. It is here that we at once pray "Lord, have mercy!" and at the same time "Lord, give us boldness that we may speak (or act) as we ought to!" It is in the prayers of the community of repentance that we come to understand, not only the tangled motives in us individually, but, by the Holy Spirit, to perceive the liberating grace of God. We, likewise, begin to experience the liberating grace of God as we seek redemptive relationships with each other. And finally, the Holy Spirit, in the prayers of the community of repentance, enables us to walk as the children of light with less and less conformity to the world, and yet with more of the telling effect that we are to have as salt and light in the world.

It is this life of repentance that gives credibility to our profession of faith. It is in the repentance unto life that we appear before the world as light in the darkness. It is by this individual and communal discipline of repentance that we stand forth in *this age* as the *people of the age to come,* the kingdom of God. True repentance breeds radical kingdom behavior!

I should not have to explicate any further how this is critical to the task of evangelization.

A word of explanation is due here before we proceed to the next point of consideration in experiencing the joyous news of the kingdom. We tend to think of an order or sequence in these matters, such as the idea that first a person inquires, then repents, etc. But that is not necessarily the way it works. It is difficult to dogmatize. I say this because some persons come to an immediate position of faith, only to inquire into its meaning later on. With many the acts of inquiry, repentance, and faith are nearly simultaneous, while with others years may separate the initiation of inquiry from the act of faith.

The Christian life is very much like the kingdom. It may be genuinely initiated by faith and baptism, yet it is always in process. By the Holy Spirit we are always inquiring afresh, finding new areas of repentance, and experiencing new vistas of the life in Christ. And we know that this is just the "down payment" of our faith, which will come to glorious consummation when Jesus returns at the end of the age. Praise God for his grace! This growth process is of him; it is his working. It is not false modesty to acknowledge the mystery of faith at this point! So let us move on in our discussion from repentance to faith.

CHAPTER 9

The Experience of Faith
in the Community of Faith

If I were a detached scholar I might be able to approach this matter of spiritual formation with a bit more theological certainty; but, having been a practicing pastor for twenty-five years and more, I have become chastened a bit. There are evangelical Christians who will assert that a Christian grows by getting alone with God in Bible study and prayer. Other Christians will say that a Christian grows in the context of the church and the sacraments.

Now there are some embarrassing dilemmas involved here. I have not seen many Christians grow healthily apart from Christian communities. But then I have seen a lot of Christians who did not grow healthily in a Christian community either. All congregations (I'm still using church, community, and congregation synonymously) are incomplete and imperfect. I think the apostles established that fact in their writings. Congregations can stray from the truth and become near nothing in their Christian expression. Solitary Christians tend to become eccentric and unfocused. But then some congregations become eccentric and unfocused too.

And yet every evangelist or ordinary Christian concerned to share the joyous news of Jesus Christ needs a Christian community. We need it as a support base. We need it as a place to depart from and return to, either in victory or defeat, to share our successes and our failures. We need it as a place of prayer and confession. We need it as a family to which we refer inquirers and into which we bring the newborn babes in Christ.

What has God given to us as a lodestar, a guidon, or a plumb line to keep us individually and corporately in harmony with himself and his purpose? What kind of given standards do we have to keep us from being more eccentric than we need to be, to keep us from zooming off on endless tangents, and to enable us to express our kingdom life with integrity?

It is these dilemmas and these questions that bring us to the whole area of *faith.* I want to describe faith as a commitment to the truth as it is made known in Jesus Christ and his holy scriptures—just that simple. We are believing people, people of truth, people of faith. That truth into which we believe is God's Son, our Savior Jesus Christ. He is the Truth. He is the author and finisher of our faith (i.e., the instigator and the perfecter). He puts his stamp of authority on the scriptures of the Old Testament. And it is he and his message that are central to the message of the apostles in the New Testament.

We have attempted to establish in earlier chapters that the overarching and all-encompassing theme of Jesus' preaching is the kingdom of God, the joyous news of the kingdom. We have sought to spell out that the church is the community of the King, or the community of the kingdom. It follows here that the word of the King, or the word of God, becomes normative for the people of the kingdom of God. Once again, though, we discover that the word of God is not cold data or sterile fact. Jesus is the Word made flesh, the Word incarnate. He personally is God's message, God's good news. Again, God has made known his own being and his will through the writings of Moses and the prophets, the Old Testament. The apostles, writing by the Holy Spirit, also claim that what they are saying is the word of God.

In all of this there is the marvel of God making known his saving purpose to his creation. The word is described as "living and active" (Heb. 4:12) because it is the revealing word of the living God. It discerns, it convicts, it makes alive, it enlightens. The purpose of the word of God, incarnate and written, is to make known the will and purpose and character of the Lord God. The Lord has spoken. He has made known the *facts* of his gospel; he has made known the *demands* of the gospel; he has made known the *promises* of the gospel; and he has called into being the *community* of the gospel, which is the church.

The community of the kingdom of God is a community of truth. God has made that truth known in his Son and in the holy scriptures. When the church or the individual Christian wanders off into eccentricity it is because there is a straying from the truth. But this truth is not just knowledge. It is also the appropriation of the truth and the obedience to the truth. To *believe* the gospel and to *obey* the gospel are nearly synonymous in New Testament writings. In the Sermon on the Mount, Jesus makes plain that the wise person is the one who hears the word of God and does it. The foolish person, conversely, is the person who only hears. The Great Commission underscores that the mandate of the Christian community is to go everywhere teaching people *to observe,* or practice, everything that Jesus has commanded.

Example of the New Testament Community

Right away, as soon as the Spirit of God has called several thousand persons to faith in Jesus the Messiah at Pentecost, what do they do? They gather publicly and in private homes to spend time in the apostles' doctrine, that is, the things the apostles had seen and heard in their fellowship with Jesus. The content of that doctrine is set forth lucidly in their writings. Soon that word spreads. The truth goes down the streets and over the back fences, as Christians cannot contain the good news but have to tell it, to explain it to the people they meet.

Then there is that whole account that we have from the pen of Luke, The Acts of the Apostles, of how the community of truth spread from Jerusalem to Rome. We find Philip, then Peter, then Paul breaking through barriers of culture and tradition as the truth and the experience of truth send forth those who are possessed by that truth. At the end of Acts we find Paul on his way to Rome, where there is already a community of faith by the time he arrives. And for two years he is in Rome teaching the kingdom of God.

See how single-minded the apostles were. It is difficult to

read the New Testament epistles and escape the thrill and excitement of the truth of Jesus Christ. In the midst of all kinds of hassles, hostility, persecution, destructive heresies, and you-name-it difficulties experienced by the churches, the apostles pointed them back to the very plain teachings of the Lord Jesus, the mandates of the kingdom of God.

The basic confession of the New Testament Christians was "Jesus is Lord!" The whole concept of the kingdom of God rests upon the advent of the Lord, the King. This being so, it is only natural for the Christian community to focus on a continual study of Jesus: his life, his teachings, his work, his will for the present, and his promises for the future. He does not will to be trusted in ignorance. The apostles let it be known that there are some things that are basic, and they call those things "the milk" that newborn babies in the faith drink. But they encourage the Christians to go on to "solid meat." Milk would be things to be understood such as repentance, faith, and baptism. Moving on to solid meat would make one strong and mature, and would mean understanding such concepts as the high priestly work of Christ (Heb. 5:11—6:20).

Fog in the Church

There was no baptizing of agnosticism with respectability in the New Testament. Paul, in stern words, denounced any who would preach any other gospel. Occasionally today one hears error or uncertainty or agnosticism justified under the guise of "pluralism in the church." Not so in the New Testament. Oh, to be sure, there is a valid pluralism in the church. There is a diversity of gifts; there is pluralism in mission and form. But there is no pluralism in the essential message, in the content of the gospel.

When the early Christians differed they searched the scriptures, they consulted the apostles, they prayed and called upon the ascended Lord to enable them to be convinced of the right way. Christians were promised a certainty of faith and of inclusion into God's family. Somehow in recent times the promise of the assurance of salvation has fallen into disrepute, as though there were something presumptive about it. Such a wandering from the confidence of faith, along with an erroneous concept of pluralism, is part of the eccentricity which we fall into when we depart from the truth which God has given us.

I regret to admit that we theologians are responsible for all too much "fog" in the church. Theological vogues and fads come along at such a clip that one can hardly keep up with them. Then the press and media report on them as though the whole church were enamored of them and predict all kinds of developments from them. Immature persons grasp onto these without discernment, and away we go. This very fact lays upon us the urgency of using scripture as that tool which God has given us to discern between light and darkness, between truth and error, between a clear atmosphere of God's revelation to us and the fog of human philosophies which mix truth and error. Each generation needs to discern the fog as it comes in many guises.

The truth of Jesus Christ is probably more frequently fogged in the church by preoccupation with externals. I have been in congregations where Jesus Christ is a complete stranger to the members of the church, yet on the walls and in the stained glass windows are all the symbols of the faith. In the worship the words of the liturgy are read and the hymns sung. What has happened to such congregations? Perhaps they have become preoccupied with the externals, with their fellowship with each other, with the building program, the altar guild, the personality of the pastor, or the church bowling league—and have forgotten what they are about. They have become eccentric and unfocused because they have drifted away from the truth.

One of the blessings of the community of the kingdom of God is that it is a community, a new family, where truth is known, and where truth dispels the fog and brings light into the darkness. It is the experience of the truth of Jesus Christ that causes us to grow into his likeness. And as this occurs, the abundant life which he promised excites us afresh with the wonder of his saving love.

Over the Threshold and into the Household of Faith

I believe that behind much evangelistic inertia there can be found a restiveness or uncertainty about one's personal state of Christian faith, or, if not that, then an uneasiness about the kind of spiritual midwifery that is necessary to assist another person out of unbelief and into faith. Let's stop here long enough then to give some very basic understanding of how one enters into the household of faith. Basic to this discussion is the simple understanding that Jesus, personally, is the door into the Father's house. He is the entrance into the kingdom of God. It is through faith in him that we obtain eternal life. Everything we will say hereafter, whether personal, experiential, or institutional, all rests upon this assumption about Jesus Christ.

I have found that there are four themes in the New Testament preaching of the gospel that assist me greatly in understanding true faith and in helping others into the faith. They are as follows:

The Data of the Faith

I believe a person can come to faith by the simple hearing of John 3:16. But the New Testament evangelists wrote their Gospels (Matthew, Mark, Luke, and John) to put the data of Jesus Christ out in plain language so that a person can understand the nature of the problem, which is sin. One Christian called the Bible "the book that understands me." The information about my own need comes through clearly in the New Testament gospels. Then the writers are eager to explain who Jesus is, what claims he made for himself, what he promised to do for us, how he died on the cross as the penalty for your sins and mine, and how he rose again in confirmation of all his claims of divinity and of salvation for us.

It is healthy to spend time in a serious reading of at least one New Testament Gospel, so that we understand the factual basis of our faith in Jesus Christ. It is time well spent to study a Gospel such as Mark or John with a person who is on the threshold of faith to be sure he or she understands what Jesus Christ is all about: his life, teachings, death on the cross, and resurrection. This information is foundational for the demands which Jesus makes.

The Demands of the Faith

The joyous news of Jesus Christ and his kingdom is not without cost. Jesus tells us to count the cost before we sign on. He warns us before we start that the way is very narrow and straight. We know that while Jesus calls us as sinners, with all our guilt and tangled up values, he certainly does not intend to leave us that way. On the basis of who we are and who he is, then, he makes at least two clear demands of us that require a moral choice, the exercise of our wills.

The first of these is *repentance*. We have spent time on this in the last chapter. Yet one demand of the faith is that we come clean about our part in the problem. We are part of the darkness. We are sinners. There is nothing anonymous about this. Repentance insists that we accept a radical new way of life under the Lordship of Jesus Christ. We deliberately turn from all that is of the darkness, all the values and allegiances, and we turn to the Light, who is Jesus Christ, and to the dominion of light, which is the kingdom of God.

The second of these demands is that we *believe*. To believe in Jesus Christ and to believe in the joyous news of the kingdom of God are essentially the same demand. In Jesus the kingdom is manifest. He is the way into the kingdom. He is the new and living way into the Father's forever family. It is his saving, gracious reign that we are believing *into*. Belief, or faith, in New Testament terms, is an activity that takes persons out of themselves and unites them with Christ. Thus, in New Testament language, one does not just believe *in*, one believes *into* Jesus Christ. It is that act whereby I yield myself up to be possessed by the one who is the object of my belief, even Jesus Christ. I trust him, and give myself to him as Savior from the ravages of sin and the guilt thereof; and I give myself to him as Lord of all, and to a new life under his Lordship.

A third demand is that of *baptism*. The Great Commission

speaks of the requirement of baptism (Matt. 28:19), as does Peter in his Pentecost sermon (Acts 2:38). This requirement has to do with publicly entering into the community of the Lord's people; it is the rite of entrance into the Christian faith and the community of faith. Let's acknowledge it and hold it until a bit later.

When one speaks of these as demands, which they are, then one also must recognize that they are the demands of God's grace and love. It is because the kingdom of God is of such surpassing value that one is called upon to repent and believe. To use the figures of the parables, the kingdom is like a treasure hid in a field, or a pearl of great price, for which a person will gladly divest himself of every other possession to acquire it. And God enables us to see, and to repent, and to believe. As he demands, he also gives grace. I do not understand how that works, nor do you. But it is certainly true.

> For by grace you have been saved through faith; and this is not your own doing, it is the gift of God—not because of works, lest any man should boast.
>
> (Eph. 2:8–9)

The Promises of the Faith

Here the extravagant grace and love of God for sinners are made known. Calling us again to himself in repentance and faith, he then makes known to us that while we were yet aliens, rebels, guilty sinners, and lost—while all that was true—Christ died for us, to deal with our guilt and with the just wrath of God, so that we might be pronounced acceptable to God as his dear children. In the promises of God we have the redemptive character of God set forth in all of its splendor. Who would have thought? It is the love of God which surpasses knowledge. It becomes the more marvelous the longer we look at it. Here is forgiveness of our sins. Here is participation in the resurrection life of Jesus Christ by the indwelling of the Holy Spirit. Here is adoption into God's family with such access and intimacy that we call him "Daddy" (cf. "Abba," Rom. 8:15–17) and are fellow heirs with Christ. Here is the promise of eternal life. Death is no longer an enemy. The deep hungerings and thirstings for acceptance and meaning are fulfilled in Jesus Christ, who is the bread of life and the water of life. Here is one who is touched with the feeling of our infirmity, who has been tempted in all points as we are, who now makes continual prayers of intercession in the Father's very presence for us. We become his dear children. He puts his name upon us.

To comprehend the love of God is a lifelong and never ending study, which can only bring us to adoration, thanksgiving, greater devotion, and ceaseless praise.

The Community of Faith

As we noted above, the call to baptism is a call into *community*. There are not the graphic passages in the New Testament which call us into community such as there are for repentance and faith. But the New Testament never conceives of Christians apart from the household of faith. The gospel is preached, persons respond, they are gathered into small churches, elders are appointed to care for the church, and a community of faith is established. Believers gather together, sharing life, studying the apostles' doctrines and the scriptures, praying, caring for each other. This is the setting of faith. Baptism appears to be the rite of entrance into that community. Through the water of baptism we give expression to our new being, our entrance into God's new covenant people, our cleansing from the defilement of sin, our regeneration.

By the twentieth century we have added so much baggage to this idea of community that it is often difficult to speak of the Christian community without raising so many questions that one is intimidated into silence. Here are scores of denominational traditions with all the requirements of bishops, associations, church courts, and missionary agencies. Does a congregation need duly ordained "clergy" to be a true church? Who can administer baptism and the Lord's Supper? Here are house churches and cathedrals, huge assemblies and isolated thatched-roof chapels. Many forms. Are all valid? Some? How does the community of the kingdom express itself? A presbytery sees an area of need and grants permission to an ordained person to go and establish a new Presbyterian congregation in one place. In another a zealous layperson sees a need and gathers Christians into his own home and teaches scripture, and they become a congregation. In Latin America a Pentecostal farmer hears of a village without the gospel and walks miles to that village each week and preaches and gathers believers into a community of faith. Which is the most valid?

The point is that in the mystery of God's working all of these congregations have been used in the spread of the gospel. Some that may be the most pure doctrinally may also be the most moribund spiritually, and some that may have all kinds of troublesome doctrines may be alive to Jesus Christ and growing. How do you explain or justify this?

In the New Testament faith, persons who desire to be part of the kingdom of God are expected to join with other believers in a community of faith. And all believers and all communities of believers are part of the body of Christ, which is his church. All belong to each other and bear responsibility for the rest of the body. This reality is part of our gospel, part of our faith. The community of the kingdom manifests itself in a great diversity of forms, but they are all God's people. We are called upon to be part of God's people, and not to forsake meeting with the community as part of our Christian discipline and growth (Heb. 10:23–25).

Baptism into the Community of Faith

It is altogether possible that baptism has become so perfunctory in the minds of many that it has lost its telling impact as a step, a dramatic step, in spiritual formation and Christian growth. To be baptized into the name of the Father, the Son, and the Holy Spirit is to come into the family of God and become an heir of God and a joint heir with Christ. That's something! It is a celebration, a most remarkable occasion in Christian experience. And in the concept of the gospel of the kingdom it is a graphic stage, when one publicly declares oneself no longer part of the darkness but a child of the light, sharing life with the people of light. It will be enough here to quote from the adult baptismal formula of the Episcopal church, which comes from the form of a very early Christian baptismal ceremony, to see how meaningful baptism is intended to be.

> *Minister.* Well-beloved, you have come hither desiring to receive holy Baptism. We have prayed that our Lord Jesus Christ would vouchsafe to receive you, to release you from sin, to sanctify you with the Holy Ghost, to give you the kingdom of heaven, and everlasting life.
>
> Dost thou renounce the devil and all his works, the vain pomp and glory of the world, with all covetous desires of the same, and the sinful desires of the flesh, so that thou wilt not follow, nor be led by them?
> *Answer.* I renounce them all; and, by God's help, will endeavor not to follow, nor be led by them.

(See what a clear statement of repentance is called forth here.)

> *Minister.* Dost thou believe in Jesus the Christ, the Son of the Living God?
> *Answer.* I do.
> *Minister.* Dost thou accept him, and desire to follow him as thy Saviour and Lord?
> *Answer.* I do.
> *Minister.* Dost thou believe all the Articles of the Christian Faith, as contained in the Apostles' Creed?
> *Answer.* I do.

(And here the act of faith, or belief, on the basis of the data of the faith is called forth.)

> *Minister.* Wilt thou be baptized in this Faith?
> *Answer.* That is my desire.
> *Minister.* Wilt thou then obediently keep God's holy will and commandments, and walk in the same all the days of thy life?
> *Answer.* I will, by God's help.

There follow here a number of prayers and statements indicating the dramatic deliverance out of the dominion of sin and into the community of redemption, which is indicated by this rite of baptism. The person is then dipped in water

or water is poured on the person. Then this statement by
the minister:

> We receive this person into the congregation of Christ's
> flock; and do sign (here the Minister shall make a Cross
> upon the person's forehead) *him* with the sign of the
> Cross, in token that hereafter *he* shall not be ashamed to
> confess the faith of Christ crucified, and manfully to fight
> under his banner, against sin, the world, and the devil;
> and to continue Christ's faithful soldier and servant unto
> *his* life's end. Amen.
>
> Seeing now, dearly beloved brethren, that *this Person* is
> regenerate, and grafted into the body of Christ's Church,
> let us give thanks unto Almighty God for these benefits;
> and with one accord make our prayers unto him, that *this*
> *Person* may lead the rest of *his* life according to this
> beginning.

(The Lord's Prayer is said by the community.)

> We yield thee hearty thanks, most merciful Father, that
> it hath pleased thee to regenerate *this* thy *Servant* with
> thy Holy Spirit, to receive *him* for thine own *child,* and
> to incorporate *him* into thy holy Church. And humbly
> we beseech thee to grant, that *he,* being dead unto sin,
> may live unto righteousness, and being buried with
> Christ in his death, may also be *partaker* of his resurrec-
> tion; so that finally, with the residue of thy holy Church,
> *he* may be *an inheritor* of thine everlasting kingdom;
> through Christ our Lord. *Amen.* [4]

I like that. Just reading through it is a blessing. It has substance. It avoids the casual, ho-hum performance of baptism
that is so much a part of our evangelical malaise. For a pastor
or another Christian just to sit down with the candidate for
baptism, or with a Christian inquirer, and discuss this baptismal
formula would be an evangelizing experience. And each time
the community shared in a baptismal service, all members
would be refreshed in the knowledge of who they are as God's
people. It is a shame to sandwich a baptism in between the
second hymn and the announcements of the congregation. Baptism is worthy of a whole season of worship. It is a fitting entrance into the community of faith.

A PERSONAL NOTE TO MY READERS

Will you allow me to probe you with a very telling question? As you have read the above baptismal formula, as you have seen the question which the minister asks and the responses given by the candidate for baptism, do you have the confidence that you have taken this private and public step of faith? Have you, as a mature person, thoughtfully and willingly stepped over the threshold of repentance and faith, thereby deliberately forsaking the dominion of sin and darkness and entering into the dominion of God's dear Son, into the household of faith?

If you ask yourself if you *fully* understand the gospel, if your repentance is *complete,* and if your faith is *strong,* the answer will be "no." You may sense your own weakness, pride, fickleness, guilt, and uncertainty. But if you know enough to know that you want to be delivered out of the darkness and into God's marvelous light, if you are willing to yield yourself up to be possessed by the gracious Lord who came to seek and to save sinners, *then* you know enough to commit all you know of yourself to all you know of him, and to rest on his word of promise: The person ". . . who comes to me I will not cast out" (John 6:37).

If you have not taken this step, with all the personal, social, and communal implications of it, then heed the Savior's "Come unto me" now. Make it known to your pastor or to your Christian community with rejoicing. Everything else in this book is secondary until you are secure in the experience of the joyous news of Jesus Christ.

R.T.H.

The Evangelizing Moment for Covenant Children

I am of the Reformed tradition of Christendom. We believe in the baptism of infant children. I know that this is a very controversial doctrine. It has evidently been practiced since sometime in the third or fourth century. It has also been debated through all the intervening centuries. In this century it has been challenged afresh by some of the dominant voices in the theological world. Be that as it may, infant baptism is practiced widely and has been practiced by the major traditions of Christendom. I only raise the issue here for the purposes of this whole section. If spiritual formation has to do with the care and feeding of God's kingdom people, and if countless thousands of these kingdom people have been baptized in infancy and have grown up within the kingdom community with all of its blessings—then there is a practical question: Is there an evangelizing moment when these "covenant children," baptized in infancy, have to look at the alternatives of darkness and light and make a moral decision, one that has the same drama as that of the adult candidate for baptism in the baptismal formula related above?

I don't think we need be defensive about that question. It will say something to us about the character of that which we call "confirmation." When a non-Christian person comes to the point of repentance, then that person looks at the character of the dominion of darkness as over against the dominion of God's dear Son and consciously and deliberately makes a choice. But the parents of a covenant child bring the infant to baptism and into the Christian community without the conscious, intelligent, and moral involvement of that infant. Does that practice, then, deprive that person of the conscious, intelligent, and moral drama of looking at the alternatives and making a choice? I think not. Yet so-called "confirmation class," where the vows of parents are ostensibly confirmed in the covenant child, is so often an automatic, perfunctory, mindless ecclesiastical puberty rite which comes just before Easter when one is eleven or twelve years old.

Look at the example of Jesus. He was of godly parents. His mother is one of the greatest examples of faith in history. He was circumcised according to the law, and taken to the temple at twelve (Bar Mitzvah?). His knowledge of the scriptures is a testimony to his home as well as to his divine and human natures. He was baptized by his cousin, John the Baptizer, and affirmed as God's well-beloved Son by a voice from heaven. What then? In the wilderness he was confronted with all the wiles of the kingdom of Satan, the allurements of the flesh, and the glamor of this present world. At that point Jesus had to decide between the will of the Father, which involved a cross, and the temptations to participate in the darkness. It was a clear moral confrontation. He chose the word of God, the will of God, and the honor of God. Then the evangelist Luke records: "Jesus returned in the power of the Spirit into Galilee . . ." (Luke 4:14).

I believe that the children of believing parents ought to be the most evangelized and the most knowledgeable and radical of kingdom people. They have had all the benefits of the community in the Holy Spirit from birth. Why are they so often so much less than this? I believe that it is because they have never been confronted with the moral choice between darkness and light. We assume that they have an affinity for the light, when too often they are fascinated by the darkness. You know the story, the church kid who becomes the "hell-raiser" as soon as he leaves home.

I believe that confirmation should not be nearly so perfunctory or so early. Covenant children ought to be made aware of the two kingdoms. And at some point in full adolescence, not before high school, they ought to be taken back to the baptismal font (figuratively at the door of the church) and, like Jesus, shown the alternatives offered by the kingdom of darkness, the other gospels of this age—hedonism, consumerism, secularism, humanism, and the rest—and called upon to make a choice! I do not think it should be programmed. The Christian community should assure them of support and love and counsel. But the rite of confirmation should be for them a decision knowledgeably made to identify publicly with the kingdom people of

God in personal confirmation of baptismal vows taken for them years before, with all the drama of that moment.

Peradventure that covenant child chooses the dominion of darkness, as many do, I do not think that renders the promises of God to parents invalid. At least the covenant child is aware of the alternatives and of the consequences of each. The Christian community is alerted to the spiritual struggle going on and is called to prayer. And the covenant-keeping God has his own ways of bringing his wandering sheep back into his fold, perhaps a bit scarred but wiser for it all. He is faithful.

Confirmation should be the evangelizing moment for covenant children. It should make the demands and promises of gospel graphic, and should contain all the drama of adult profession of faith. Every generation of Christians needs that moment and should be the stronger for it!

The Community of Faith as a Community of the Word of God

God's kingdom people mature as they "marinate" in the knowledge of the scriptures. A Christian congregation should be a people of scriptures. A biblically illiterate and mindless community of Christians is a scandal. This doesn't mean that Christian people need to be highly educated and scholarly. But it does mean that they should know what God has said and done. Scripture should be prominent in a kingdom community. There is nothing wrong with a congregation sponsoring a badminton team or a square dancing club, unless those peripheral activities obscure the prominence of the knowledge of the Word of God and obedience to the Word of God.

If a community of faith is going to be rich in the knowledge of the scriptures, then it almost goes without saying that every Christian ought to have a discipline of the daily study of scriptures. One's Bible study time and prayer time should grow out of each other. Bible study should be prayerful dwelling in the Word of God. Prayer should, conversely, be a response to scriptures. It is those ordinary, day-by-day times in scripture that are essential in the healthy growth of any Christian. It is this personal discipline which, when added together in the community, makes community times in scripture more profound and meaningful. Group Bible studies should be encouraged. Church schools should not allow too much "curriculum" to come between the person and the Bible. Pastors should be biblical expositors and teachers in the pulpit, and not trade on topical whims and current events.

Spiritual formation takes place and evangelism prospers in communities where the Word of God is known and obeyed. And the community of faith comes often to the Lord's Table, where the Word is made visible in the bread and the wine.

The Community of Faith as a Community of Worship

One more thing before we pass on to another dimension of experiencing the joyous news of the kingdom: the community of faith, because it is God's community where he is the reigning Sovereign, is a community of *worship*. We believe in God. We have turned to him and to his kingdom because he is worthy of our trust. He is therefore worthy of our devotion, of our prayers, and of our praise. A community of faith rejoices in God: Father, Son, and Holy Spirit. A community of faith is a thankful community, always and in all situations giving thanks. Psalms and hymns and spiritual songs abound. The soul of the Christian prospers in worship. Obedience is joyous and spontaneous as the believer dwells upon the God of salvation. The community of faith is a community rich in worship!

Epilogue

A few months ago a group of students called me up to ask if I would be a speaker at a college conference. Their request was that, using this kingdom of God theme, I should do the following: "Radicalize us, Bob. Do for us what the Marxists do for their people; give us a sense of history, of calling, of meaning, of purpose and destiny. Help us to know what it means to be the community of the kingdom of God!"

It is this kind of flavor that I trust I have initiated in this discussion of the community of faith. And now on to some other dimensions of the growth of the Christian and the community of the kingdom.

CHAPTER 10
The Character of Christ:
The Goal of Our Faith

We've been discussing here for several chapters the whole area of the Christian growth, or spiritual formation, of those who are truly experiencing the joyous news of God's kingdom. I want us to keep our focus clear as to what we are about. The theme of this book is the joyous news of the kingdom of God and how that joyous news is communicated to all the world. Critical to this ministry of communicating the joyous news is the reality of our life, experience, and growth as the people of the joyous news, the household of faith. I have been trying also to hold together both the individual and communal dimensions of our spiritual formation. If I am leaning overboard on the communal side, it is because that side appears to me to be the more neglected. The more vigorous the Christian community, the more wholesome the lives and experiences of the individual members.

We have spent substantial space on the matters of repentance and faith because these are so foundational. But there are many other factors in our spiritual formation that are no less essential if we are to be, as Paul expresses it, "the aroma of Christ to God" (2 Cor. 2:15). You see, the goal of our Christian growth is not *primarily* that we be good evangelists. The divinely stated purpose is larger than that. Perhaps it comes out most clearly in this statement from the letter to the Roman church:

> We know that in everything God works for good with those who love him, who are called according to his purpose. For those whom he foreknew he also predestined

to be conformed to the image of his Son, in order that he
might be the first-born among many brethren.
(Rom. 8:28–29, emphasis mine)

This puts the focus of God's eternal purpose on a people who
are conformed to the likeness, or character, or image, of his Son.
This indicates, then, that there is a goal to our Christian growth.
It states that the family likeness of God is to be fleshed out in
the Christian person and in the Christian community. If we are
the body of Christ, which name is given to the church, then by
all means the world has a right to observe the character of
Christ expressed in our Christian community.

I know that concept staggers the imagination. Yet, as we
evaluate our own lives and congregations, the character of
Christ should be much more in the forefront of our thinking
than budgets, buildings, programs, and activities. Where am I
going as a Christian person? Where are we going as a Christian
congregation? Are we maturing in the character of Christ? Are
we selecting elders, deacons, stewards, vestry on the basis of
their prominence in the community, or on the basis of their
maturity in the character of Christ and their proven capacity to
manifest his character in the congregation?

Let me, then, present a potpourri of characteristics that we
should have before us as those expressive of the gospel, of the
character of our Lord Jesus, of the joyous news of the kingdom
of God. These will be brief and therefore only provocative of
your study of the much larger volume of material that is behind
each one of them. Here, then, are some of the characteristics
into which we need to be consciously growing.

The Fullness of the Holy Spirit and
the Communion of the Holy Spirit

How do you explain the Christian life or the Christian
church apart from the Holy Spirit? It cannot be done. If you
consign the third person of the Trinity to a minor role at some
earlier point of history, then you do violence both to the Trinity
and to the nature of the Christian church as the "fellowship of
the Holy Spirit" (2 Cor. 13:14). There is a line from a contempo-

rary chorus which states it succinctly: "The Spirit of God was not lost after Pentecost." In no way can such a thought even be allowed—that the mighty working of the Spirit of God should have ceased after Pentecost. The ascended Lord Jesus, in fulfillment of the promise to his disciples, sent forth the Holy Spirit upon his church to enable it to live the life to which he had called it. The new life in Christ is the life indwelt by the Spirit of Christ, the Holy Spirit. The power of the age to come is the power of the third person of the Godhead dynamic in the church.

From its earliest days the church has prayed: "Veni, Creator Spiritus!" "Come, Creator Spirit!" And today we sing those wonderful prayers to the Holy Spirit: "Come Holy Spirit, Heavenly Dove"; "Spirit of God Descend Upon My Heart"; and scores of others. We are called upon always to be filled with the Holy Spirit (Eph. 5:18). The Holy Spirit is the "immeasurable" power at work within us which Paul mentions (Eph. 1:19). The gospel is not to come forth from the church simply in human words, but "in power and in the Holy Spirit and with full conviction" (1 Thess. 1:5). The Spirit gives joy and boldness. The Spirit pours out the love of God into our hearts. The Spirit of God is the Spirit who empowers and enables his new covenant people. The Spirit is to be loved and adored with the Father and the Son.

I, for one, praise God for the emergence of Pentecostalism and the "charismatic movement" in this century to remind us again of the person and work of the third person of the Trinity. Despite some of the excesses (which have given me not a few gray hairs), the awakening of the church to the promise of the Holy Spirit's working in the church is an enormous encouragement. The Christian person and the Christian community ought always be open to and praying for new invasions of the Holy Spirit, so that the life and power and expectancy, the dynamic of the kingdom of God, will be manifest among his people.

The evidence of the Holy Spirit's role in spiritual formation will be shown in those other characteristics of growing Christians which follow.

Persons with Gifts in a Community of Gifts

In my own mind, one of the greatest tragedies ever to come upon the Christian church was the exalting of a few into a class of magisterial "clergy." This ostensible breed of super-Christians clearly violates one of the remarkable biblical teachings about our communion in the Holy Spirit, namely, that every believer has a gift *(charisma)* to be used in ministry. The reformers made a half-hearted attempt to remedy some of the excesses of the priesthood by talking of the priesthood of all believers, but the idea of clergy sailed right through the Reformation uncriticized.

Four very demanding passages of scripture need to be before us as we seek to know how the ascended Lord equips his people for the calling. These passages all talk of the gifts and ministries that belong to every single member of the Christian community, bar none! They are: Romans 12:3–8; 1 Corinthians 12—14; Ephesians 4:1–16 (esp. vs. 7); 1 Peter 4:7–11. These passages need to be studied carefully. Several things emerge out of them:

1) Here is one of the most singular clues as to the structure and ministry of the New Testament church. The structure and ministry are clearly charismatic. God gives gifts and all members employ their gifts for the good of all—no arm twisting to secure members of committees and commissions. There is something beautifully spontaneous and natural about persons working together because of the energizing and gifting of the Holy Spirit.

2) Nobody is insignificant. The gifts are not a violation of one's personality. The ascended Lord gives gifts as he sees the need in the community, but he also gives the gifted persons the motivation and capacity to exercise their particular ministries with a sense of responsible stewardship before the Lord and to the community.

3) Gifts emerge and are proven in the Christian community. The other members of the community are able to

see gifts, ministries, or God-given capacities in those with whom they are associated in the close fellowship. You see this in the teaching concerning the diaconal ministry in Acts 6 and 1 Timothy 3, where deacons are expected to be manifestly and provenly those with the capacity and character to carry on this ministry.

4) The community with its elders, or bishops, has oversight of the gifts and can confirm or deny the gifts. All through the history of the church there are persons who dash into the community and say: "God told me to have this ministry, or to do these things." It is not only one of the functions of the elders to encourage and call forth the gifts of the community, but also to confirm and give order to the expression of gifts. The Christian community is not chaos or anarchy.

5) The biblical teaching also raises some hard questions about traditions having to do with leadership in the church that have been too long unquestioned. For instance, what are the criteria for leadership? What proven capacities does a person need to express to have a role of leadership? Do elders or deacons or pastors have to prove any gifts in the community? Or are they selected and ordained on the basis of personal desire or popularity? I assume that a pastor-teacher is a brother or a sister with a gift of equipping and caring, who expresses that gift in a community of other gifts. That gift shows itself, and the community has a right to set it apart for more effective use. Yet we accept unproven adolescents and process them through a three- or four-year academic curriculum, assuming that by such cerebretonic experience they are proven, and so ordain them and make them pastors, teachers, and "clergy"! What of love, wisdom, humility, character, example? What of family life? What of response to crises? The charismatic structure of the Christian community sets apart leaders on the basis of gifts that are proven in the community.

6) The gifts and ministries are interdependent. They all work together in harmony. They are all necessary for the effective functioning of the others. When one person doesn't function in stewardship of his or her gift, then there is an effect on the whole of the body. We need each other! That is the point. The most visible and prominent of the gifts may not be the most crucial to the healthy functioning of the body.

7) When every believer, every Christian, is trying to use a gift given by the Lord in the ministry of the body, then there is motivation and a sense of conscientiousness that is lacking when a person is persuaded humanly to "take a job" because "we need one more member on this committee."

8) While all Christians are called to be "witnesses" to their faith and ready to discuss it with anyone, the gift of "evangelist" is only one gift among many and is not any more crucial than any other. It is one of the more difficult gifts to define. And the evangelist can only function fruitfully as others in the community are expressing their gifts in the interdependent community.

The biblical teaching of gifts and the community of gifts liberates the laity for ministry, and makes the pastor-teacher primarily an equipper of the laity for the work of the ministry. Christians mature and Christian communities become more effective in expressing the character of the kingdom as gifts are expressed, matured, and ministered interdependently according to the scriptural pattern.

Loving Persons in a Community of Love

In Paul's letter to the Corinthian Christians, he comes to a point in the thirteenth chapter where, for all practical purposes, he equates lovelessness with immaturity. Here was a church fraught with party-spirit, which Paul says is an expression of a

purely human (i.e., non-Christian) level of conduct; with pettiness over the expression of gifts; with insensitivity at the Lord's
Table, which he says does not discern the body of Christ; as well
as with other moral problems. He is dealing with the problem
of the expression of gifts when he delivers what is both a hymn
to love and a stern rebuke to lovelessness: the thirteenth chapter of 1 Corinthians. Love, he says, always has the redemptive
welfare of the other at heart and is willing to go to any lengths
to provide ministry to the other person. This love, of course, is
the love of God wrought in our lives by the Holy Spirit. At the
climax of that passage, he states:

> When I was a child, I spoke like a child, I thought like a
> child, I reasoned like a child; when I became a man, I
> gave up childish ways.   (1 Cor. 13:11)

The point is that love expresses Christian maturity. It is in our
true Christian love that we express our kingdom behavior most
tellingly. The Corinthian Christians were showing immaturity
by their loveless behavior within the community.

It is worth pausing here for a moment to reflect on this
phenomenon. A congregation in which there is strife, indifference, gossip, group spirit, and pettiness over personal privilege
is a travesty of the gospel and of the kingdom community.

There is probably no more telling passage in the New Testament on the imperative character of love than Jesus' own words
in John 13:34–35:

> "A new commandment I give to you, that you love one
> another; even as I have loved you, that you also love one
> another. By this all men will know that you are my disci-
> ples, if you have love for one another."

First off, this is a commandment given by our Lord. That makes
it mandatory. Jesus didn't give many commandments, but here
is one. Secondly, he defines what that love is like: it is like his
love for us. That is a costly and self-effacing love; it is redemptive love. His third point has all kinds of implications pertaining
to our evangelistic impact on the world around us. All people

will be made aware that we are Christ's disciples because of this kind of love within our community. Within a few decades after the church was born, secular historians were already commenting on the love which Christians had for one another.

Such love is humanly impossible. But Paul encourages us by saying that the love of God is poured out into our hearts by the Holy Spirit (Rom. 5:5). I was in a situation a few years ago where I had some very difficult and antagonistic personalities to cope with within the Christian community. I found myself wishing they would go away, leave the church, and leave me alone. In a prayer meeting one evening some brothers and sisters asked what was my greatest need for prayer. I said that I really wanted to be able to love some persons that I found difficult to love. Several of these dear Christians laid hands on me and prayed that God would pour out his love in me by the Holy Spirit. I was astonished, for in the days that followed I had the most heartfelt and tender love for those very people that I had wished would go away. Christian love is a miracle of God's grace, a mark of the community, and a testimony to the non-Christian world.

Christian love is to be genuine. It is a love that is free to rebuke, encourage, and serve. It is through love that church leaders earn their authority, an authority based on love. Love is costly and practical. It is both tough and gentle. We love because we are loved by God. Nothing is more distressing than a person, or a community, that professes to belong to Jesus Christ and yet expresses indifference to others and lovelessness in character.

> So faith, hope, love abide, these three; but the greatest of these is love.   (1 Cor. 13:13)

Persons of Hope in a Community of Hope and Freedom

The Christian community is a community of the resurrection. Christ is risen! The powers of sin and death have been destroyed. By his cross and resurrection we have been set free. The future is unlocked. All things are possible. Hallelujah!

In the kingdom of darkness we were without hope and without God in the world. Present were alienation, bondage, fear, the oppressive presence of power structures and systems of evil that drove us to escapism, unreality, or despair.

No longer. Jesus Christ is risen. Death has lost its sting. "He disarmed the principalities and powers and made a public example of them, triumphing over them [by his cross]" (Col. 2:15). We are set free to be God's new creation, and that freedom is dynamic. We are made free in ourselves to accept ourselves as God accepts us. We are made free to love each other and to serve each other. We are made free toward God with perfect access to him, devoid even of the conscience of sin. And we are made free again to be stewards rather than spoilers of his creation.

The Spirit of God in us is the Spirit of hope and freedom.

Between the Ages: The Community of the Incarnation

A mistake that many young Christians fall into, and not a few false teachers, is thinking that, since we are the heirs of eternal life, and since the blessings we have been discussing above are our heritage, we then no longer share the plight and sufferings of the rest of humanity. One of the early errors that crept into the church was called "Docetism." In short, it was a heresy that denied the real humanity of Christ. In the view of the Docetists, Christ only appeared to be human but had not really shared in the plight of true humanity. The church quickly labeled this idea a heresy or an erroneous teaching. Yet forms of Docetism continue to appear among those who hold a view of the spiritual nature of our Christian faith.

Look at the word of Paul to the Philippian Christians:

> Have this mind among yourselves, which is yours in Christ Jesus, who, though he was in the form of God, did not count equality with God a thing to be grasped, but emptied himself, taking the form of a servant, being born in the likeness of men. And being found in human form he humbled himself. . . .   (Phil. 2:5–8)

Or at the words of Jesus:

> "I do not pray that thou shouldst take them out of the
> world, but that thou shouldst keep them from the evil
> one."
>
> (John 17:15)

In this "between the ages" period in which we live, we are
in fact the people of the kingdom, but we are also living in this
present world. We share the frailty, the sufferings, the blights
and inhumanities of the rest of humankind. Even more, we
receive the contempt and the sometime persecutions of those
who hate our God. Jesus promised us this.

And it is in this identification with suffering humanity and
in this discipline of chastening that God gives us the kind of
temper, or character, that nothing else can provide for us. The
writer of the letter to the Hebrews quotes the Proverbs to make
divine chastening almost axiomatic for the Christian: "For the
Lord disciplines him whom he loves, and chastises every son
whom he receives" (Heb. 12:6). The end result of all of this is
a perfecting work in us which God designs.

We do not grow in true character and depth by floating
along on some "spiritual high." The plight of the poor, the
diseased, the oppressed, the imprisoned, the naked, and the
hungry, which was the concern of our Lord, becomes ours and
we become servants. Christians are those who are to be more
truly human than anyone else. We are God's new covenant
humanity, his new creation. The crises, the struggles, the tribu-
lations, the inexplicable tragedies that are the lot of people in
the world are ours also. Only, we are those who know hope; we
are the Father's children. We have resources in the midst of this
tragic scene that do not belong to those who refuse God or who
don't know him. And this is a very real part of our gospel.

No small part of the church's witness to the world has been
manifested when the world has expressed its hate for us because
we belong to Christ. The testimony of Christian persons in the
face of persecution and death has very often been the beginning of a new outburst of evangelistic and missionary fervor.

This dimension of our growth into the character of Christ is more sobering; but it is the walk of faith in the fires of hardship and tribulation that produces the depth or profundity of true Christlikeness. It may be that the superficiality of much of the North American Christian church is due to the whole context of ease, wealth, success, and lack of significant opposition in which the church lives. One would hesitate to pray for chastenings, but looking at the splendid character of the Christians coming out of Latin America, Russia, Africa, and other settings of difficulty, one is almost willing to fasten one's seat-belt and pray: "Have at it, Lord!"

God's kingdom community shares in the humanity, the sufferings, of the rest of the world. Moreover, we are to expect persecutions. It is in pain that faith and hope and love are refined. It is in these experiences that we are salt and light. It is here that we are Christ's servant people.

Christ's Compassionate People

Of the many beautiful characteristics and virtues of our Lord Jesus, there is one that I want to dwell on before we come to the conclusion of this section on spiritual formation. That characteristic is *compassion*. How very compassionate was our Lord Jesus Christ. He felt deeply the lostness and the gnawing human need of those around him. He could never be accused of being insensitive. He saw whole persons, not detatched souls. He understood the interrelation of emotional, physical, spiritual, and social dimensions of people's lives. He looked upon the multitudes and hurt because they were like sheep without a shepherd. He looked upon the holy city of Jerusalem and wept because the people were so spiritually obtuse. He had the concern that if the multitude left without being fed the people might well faint on the way home, so he fed them. Even in his dying moments he looked upon the needs of his mother and gave her to John that she might be cared for.

As we think of spiritual formation, or Christian growth, we need to dwell on this expression of the mercy and grace of God.

As a father pities his children, so the Lord pities those
who fear him. For he knows our frame; he remembers
that we are dust.   (Ps. 103:14)

The author of the Hebrews epistle says that Jesus came of
the seed of Abraham so that he might be like his brethren in
every respect, so that he might become a merciful and faithful high priest in the service of God, to make expiation for
the sins of the people. Because he himself has suffered and
been tempted, he is able to help those who are tempted
(Heb. 2:16–18). This concept picks up the themes of love and
incarnation that we have discussed above. But it goes a bit
further. The word *compassion* has the connotation of a
deep, gut-level feel for another person or human situation.
Jesus wept and became angry and labored because he loved
so profoundly and felt so keenly the agony of God's rebel-
lious creation.

The Pharisees were only capable of being indignant because
their laws and traditions were violated. They seemed to have
no sorrow or grief over the tragedy of people who were without
God in the world. The spirit of the Pharisees is antithetical to
compassion. Persons who are insensitive, judgmental, imper-
sonal, unlistening, monological, and saturated with self-esteem
have not gotten the message of the King. No, our Lord Jesus,
our blessed Redeemer and Savior, is one who is compassionate.
He is the friend of sinners. He is the Lord who looks upon the
widows and orphans and cares for them. He is the one who
consorts with publicans and sinners because they are the ones
who know that their lives are fractured.

When we look at the image of God's dear Son, into which we
are being conformed, we need to take this characteristic of
compassion into account. Especially is this true as we begin to
think of the outreach of the gospel.

We, as Christ's people, need to see all people as created by
God and loved by God, though fallen and defiled. We understand what sin is all about. We have been there. But we have
also experienced the redeeming and forgiving grace of God.

We understand God's purpose and humanity's rebellion. We feel both deeply.

And because we understand all this, we also share God's outrage that his creation has been defiled. We see lives scarred by greed, by drugs, by secular values, by wicked political systems, by hatred, and by selfishness, and we are justly angry. When we see hopelessness, separation, fear, and helplessness we know that such are violations of God's true intention for his creation. "An enemy hath done this!" When we look today upon the oppression of masses of people in certain nations we hurt. When we look at despair in our American cities we are grieved. When we see our friends slowly destroying their lives and families by false values and corrupting lifestyles we are in agony.

Then, compassion does not stand aloof. Compassion does not keep its hands clean or avoid involvement. Compassion identifies with the other person, just as Jesus did in the incarnation. He shared our humanity, our temptations, our infirmities, and hence we can see his compassion for sinners. He sat and talked with them. He saw behind their masks. He knew what was inside of folks. And as he saw and felt, so must we.

Christian persons and communities that are immature in compassion are either hard on real sinners or indifferent to them. Compassion, on the other hand, compels us to practical ministry that will bring salvation in ways most desperately needed by that person or in that social situation. Ultimately, you see, our desire is to bring all things back into harmony with God through our Lord, Jesus Christ. Needed help may be abolishing an unjust law. It may be giving a cup of cold water. It may be speaking the word of the love of God in Jesus Christ that sets a burdened soul free. Such help acts because it loves and feels deeply by the Spirit of God.

Epilogue: An Imperfect Community of Imperfect People

Lest you be overwhelmed at the calling to life under the Lordship of Jesus Christ, it is always good to remember with Paul that "we have this treasure in earthen vessels, to show that the transcendent power belongs to God and not to us" (2 Cor. 4:7). Praise God that he uses clay pots to contain his glorious message and work! We are a people of grace in a community of grace. We are always imperfect and in process, yet his and under his love. The prophet Isaiah lets us know that "a bruised reed he will not break, and a dimly burning wick he will not quench" (Isa. 42:3). This word gives us the confidence that God uses sputtering, struggling people like we are to carry on his work. Yet he leads us from simple faith to more mature faith. He ushers us out of a simple experience of grace into a more profound experience of grace. "And we all, with unveiled face, beholding the glory of the Lord, are being changed into his likeness from one degree of glory to another; for this comes from the Lord who is the Spirit" (2 Cor. 3:18).

We are the Lord's. The church is the Lord's. He knows who we are. He gives grace and help to his imperfect people. It is he who is at work in us both to will and to do of his good pleasure. And so we are given heart and encouragement. Hallelujah!

With some sketchy sense of our message and of our experience and growth in the gospel of the kingdom of God, we move on now to our third section, which has to do with *obeying* the gospel of the kingdom, or *evangelism.*

SECTION 3
Obeying the Joyous News of the Kingdom of God

When anyone is united to Christ, there is a new world; the old order is gone, and a new order has already begun.

From first to last this has been the work of God. He has reconciled us . . . to himself through Christ, and he has enlisted us in this service of reconciliation. What I mean is, that God was in Christ reconciling the world to himself, no longer holding men's misdeeds against them, and that he has entrusted us with the message of reconciliation. We come therefore as Christ's ambassadors. It is as if God were appealing to you through us: in Christ's name, we implore you, be reconciled to God!

(2 Cor. 5:17–21, NEB)

CHAPTER 11
Communicating the Gospel in the Clash of Kingdoms

Actually, *obeying* the joyous news of the kingdom of God isn't all that difficult if we have thoroughly digested what has been said in sections one and two. When a person, or a congregation, *understands* and *has experienced* the joyous news of the kingdom of God, evangelization is natural and spontaneous. People cannot keep such news to themselves. Still, we'll work on some of the disciplines, or formations, that will facilitate the work of evangelization among us.

There is one awareness that we have, however, by virtue of our understanding of the coming of the kingdom of God. We understand that evangelization is the assault of the kingdom of light upon the kingdom of darkness. It involves a clash of kingdoms. We have often fallen into the trap of so wanting the acceptance of the kingdom of darkness that we have tried to wrap our message in the sophisticated dress of those whom we are addressing, so muting its radical nature. But the New Testament never lets us entertain the idea that evangelism is the picking and choosing among the offerings of several religions. We are not in the business of "conning" persons into accepting Jesus because it is good for them and better than some other religion. It may, in fact, be good for them and all of that. But our joyous news is God himself, as he has come to us in the person of Jesus of Nazareth and, through Jesus, called us into his new order, the kingdom of God. In proclaiming this news, we are putting the lie to all the false claims of the darkness. We are turning people from the power of Satan unto God.

This is conflict. It is spiritual warfare. Paul states it:

> Seeing then that we have been entrusted with this com-
> mission, which we owe entirely to God's mercy, we
> never lose heart. We have renounced the deeds that men
> hide for very shame; we neither practise cunning nor
> distort the word of God; only by declaring the truth
> openly do we recommend ourselves, and then it is to the
> common conscience of our fellowmen and in the sight of
> God. And if indeed our gospel be found veiled, the only
> people who find it so are those on the way to perdition.
> Their unbelieving minds are so blinded by the god of this
> passing age, that the gospel of the glory of Christ, who is
> the very image of God, cannot dawn upon them and
> bring them light. It is not ourselves that we proclaim; we
> proclaim Christ Jesus as Lord, and ourselves as your ser-
> vants, for Jesus' sake. For the same God who said, "Out
> of darkness let light shine," has caused his light to shine
> within us, to give the light of revelation—the revelation
> of the glory of God in the face of Jesus Christ.
>
> (2 Cor. 4:1-6, NEB)

Get it very clearly into your minds. In the coming of Jesus
into human history, the kingdom of God is inaugurated.
Through his life, death, and resurrection a new and living way
is opened into the Father's family. Through him a people is
called, a church is built. This people, which is his body, living
under his gracious and saving Lordship, under his sovereign
will, is a people committed to praying and working that his will
may be done on earth as in heaven, that his kingdom may be
realized among us.

As is stated in the scripture above, we are God's servant
people whose task it is to proclaim this message. We want to
make known in every way possible that Jesus is Lord. We are
God's ambassadors, with the full authority of heaven, sent to
implore men and women to be reconciled to God through Jesus
Christ.

In saying all of this, however, we are acknowledging the
very real existence of the dominion of darkness. We discussed
this idea in chapter one, but it is worth repeating. This dominion of darkness and the persons who are part of this dominion

are all participants in systems of evil, philosophies that deny the character and will of the Creator God. There are all of the forces of injustice and oppression. There are the false agendas of this passing age, and all of the false solutions and messiahs. The people who walk in darkness are continually fabricating panaceas for their problems. Behind all of this is the god of this world, the prince of darkness, who is Satan.

What this means is that we must be aware of the spiritual conflict involved in evangelism. To ignore this conflict is to be as foolish as the young person who looks at the recruiting poster that promises adventure, travel, and education when one joins the military. Then when, having joined, he finds that he is being shot at, he is surprised and alarmed and feels that he was recruited under false pretenses. Evangelism involves a clash of values and of authorities.

Every time the word of the kingdom of God enters an ear, every time a person exercises mind and will and so yields allegiance to Jesus Christ as Lord, and every time the Lord's Prayer is prayed there is a conflict between the power of Satan and that of our Lord Jesus Christ. And, in the broadest sense, evangelization takes place. As the community of the kingdom of God, we evangelize as we demonstrate our kingdom life and our kingdom values. We evangelize when we express in life the character and will of our heavenly Father.

In this section, however, we want to focus on the discipline of *evangelization* as we find it in the New Testament. In the New Testament this word is used to speak of that deliberate enterprise of Christian persons, and of the Christian community, whose purpose is to bring others to repentance and faith, to baptism and inclusion in the Christian fellowship. It has to do with the faithful communication of the New Testament gospel which enables folks to believe.

In the section on "Understanding the Joyous News of the Kingdom," we spoke to this matter of faithful communication in explicating the signs of the age to come. We spoke of the church as a sign, and we spoke of holiness of life as a sign. Those realities do in fact have a function in evangelization. They catch the attention of the persons who are part of the darkness. They are, as classically defined, preparations for evangelism. In this section we will not rehearse those signs; we will assume them. But we will talk of the behavior of the Christian community and of the Christian person that is explicitly evangelistic.

We live "between the ages." Both the dominion of darkness and the dominion of light are present. This is the arena of our life and witness. The future has invaded the present. The age to come has come upon this passing age. God's kingdom is dynamically, though imperfectly and incompletely, present. God's church is his dwelling place by the Spirit and is a sign of the age to come. God's people living out his will and character are a sign of the age to come and are his agents of righteousness. Yet the conflict rages. To use the figures of the book of Revelation, the Beast is at war with the Lamb and seeking to destroy the saints of God. Their prayer goes up: "How long, O Lord?" There is always the eroding influence of this age, the tendency to be conformed to the world (Rom. 12:2). Yet at the same time there is the gracious working of the Holy Spirit strengthening his people with might in their daily lives (Eph. 3:16) and making them alive to the wisdom, love, and grace of God.

Countless communities of Christian people in all the centuries have been signs of the kingdom to their generations. These may be the "two or three gathered in Christ's name" or they may be huge congregations or movements that are more visible. We only want to have clearly in our minds what we are up to in the work of evangelization. We are heralding the joyous news of the kingdom of our God to those who are still part of the darkness. We are calling them through Jesus Christ into the kingdom of God and, specifically, into those communities that are the communities of the kingdom where we live together in his grace and under his Lordship by the power of the Holy Spirit.

Despite the spiritual conflict, our message is one of joy to the world. Our Lord has come! In him is hope, meaning, love, forgiveness, acceptance, and the power of new life. He has come to make all things new. He has come to bring salvation to his lost creation. We must never let that joyous news be obscured.

We are not trading on our experience in itself, but on our experience of him, the Lord.

The immutable message of every Christian and of the whole of Christ's church is that Jesus is Lord, and that in him and through him the manifest reign of God among us is now a dynamic reality. Whether people receive us or not, the reality of God's kingdom is unchanged. Our hope is undiminished. The Spirit of God in us keeps producing the fruits, or evidences, of our kingdom life, notwithstanding the assaults of darkness.

We see history, current events, cultural patterns, and social movements through the perspective of the word of our King. Because we love him, because our joy is in him, because of our indebtedness to him, we are therefore seeking in every way possible to make the gospel of the kingdom known. We are willing to appear foolish and reckless. We become all things to all persons that we might by all means see them partake of God's salvation (1 Cor. 9:22).

An illustration of this attitude comes from Berkeley, California. Berkeley has been the scene of some of the major radical social protests. It is also the scene of one of the foremost universities in the United States. The pastor of a prominent congregation near the campus relates with a touch of humor and chagrin how for years his congregation tried to influence the campus for Christ. They used endowed lectureships and brought forth outstanding intellects who were spokespersons for the Christian faith. Yet it all had little apparent effect. But in the early 1970's in the midst of all the radical protests there emerged a group of Christians who forsook safety and propriety and went to the streets in a radical Christian witness. There they were, in the beards and overalls of that particular milieu, but engaging the non-Christians with a boldness and an enthusiasm and an effectiveness that became a milestone in recent evangelistic history.

The pastor of that nearby church says, in retrospect, that after all of their sophisticated efforts, "who influenced the University of California for Christ? Not us. It was those rambunctious street Christians who were willing to be made fools for Christ!"

I knew those "rambunctious street Christians." They weren't hiding behind their sense of propriety or behind their pulpits. They were there, incarnate in the middle of the conflict over lives on Sproul Plaza at the University of California. They knew the cultural setting and challenges. They knew the bondage of those lives apart from Christ. They saw the false gospels of the activist movements and the cults. So with great zeal for God, and intense preparation in prayer, Bible study, knowledge of the setting, and mutual support, they moved out with the joyous news of the kingdom of God. There was something refreshingly biblical about their witness. There were perils and threats of bodily harm. There was the very normal human fear and trepidation over the consequences of what they were doing. But God gave a boldness and a creativity that was greatly used. They became all things to all people that they might at all costs save some. These street Christians had been delivered from the darkness. They had enormous compassion for those still in it. These Christians had forsaken the safety of their community sanctuary and had gone out to seek and to save the lost.

But what was even more thrilling was that the compassionate character of their community was noised abroad. It was not an unusual thing for really fractured persons to seek out the Christian community in its times of sharing and prayer, hoping to find there the answers that these Christians seemed to have. And when they found the community, they found Christians who were very aware of their calling, of their gospel, and of their ministry of evangelism. Even times of Bible study and prayer became evangelistic, as curious and needy persons came into the community to look and listen, and to inquire.

I raise this episode as an example and an illustration. As God's community of joyous news, we need to ask the simple questions:

> What kind of Christian impact do we want to make in our locality?
> Who are the specific persons we want to reach for Jesus Christ?
> Where is there darkness where we want to bring light?

How am I (or are we) going to implement the answers to these questions?

Who is equipping our community for this work?

What kind of changes do we need to make in our priorities to see this happen?

What will it take to enable us to become creatively, joyously, aggressively the people of the joyous news of the kingdom of God?

If we really intend to be this kind of people, and to implement the answers to these questions, then it is not all that hard to do. What follows are some biblical patterns and principles that are often overlooked in the work of evangelization. Our goal, after all, is that we be a community that is spontaneously evangelistic. We are not looking for a program, but for a way of life that is contagious with the joyous news. So, here goes!

CHAPTER 12
The Gospel on Display

Did you ever ask yourself where a non-Christian person would find a sample of the Christian faith? Did you ever think what a demand we are putting on the credulity of non-Christians when we ask them to believe (a) that there is a God, (b) who is personal, (c) who has come to us in time and space, (d) who loves us and has called us to turn to him and be saved, (e) who has established a new order that transcends the passing order of this present world, and (f) who indwells his people by the supernatural power of the Holy Spirit?

Face it! That's a lot to swallow. I was made embarrassingly aware of this on one occasion. A group of us were "sharing Christ" (as we spoke of our ventures in evangelism) in a large city park among a large number of transient youth culture folk. My teammate and I were having a particularly positive conversation with a group of young adults. After about forty-five minutes of conversation and an established sense of friendliness, one of the young men said: "Bob, you're a Christian. We know that. We like you. But don't give us anymore of that 'God loves you' stuff. How do we know that? People have been saying that to us all across the country. Show us something. Show us where the love of God is!"

That was a legitimate challenge. If our gospel is not demonstrable, then we're just hustling words. "Eternal life" begins when we believe into Christ, not at some future after death. And that eternal life, that new life by the Spirit, must evidence itself here and now. The gospel must be demonstrable.

And this brings us to a significant New Testament principle. Please look carefully at this! In the letters to the churches, the epistles of the New Testament, you will search in vain for much teaching on the work of evangelization. Check it out! You will find the apostle speaking of his own sense of responsibility to reach people with the gospel. There is one statement in the tenth chapter of Romans which speaks of the necessity of the heralding of the gospel if people are to hear it. But it is a unique passage. If evangelism is as important as we present-day evangelicals make it out to be, then one would think that it would be a recurring theme in the letters to the young churches. But not so!

How does one explain this? It is unthinkable that the apostles were encouraging the churches to be indifferent to the people around who were still of the darkness.

The clue comes in a category of scriptural passages such as the following, which abound in the epistles:

> Maintain good conduct among the Gentiles, so that in case they speak against you as wrongdoers, *they may see* your good deeds and glorify God on the day of visitation.
> (1 Pet. 2:12, emphasis mine)

> Do all things without grumbling or questioning, that you may be blameless and innocent, children of God without blemish in the midst of a crooked and perverse generation, among whom you shine as lights in the world.
> (Phil. 2:14–15)

> Conduct yourselves wisely toward outsiders, making the most of the time. Let your speech always be gracious, seasoned with salt, so that you may know how you ought to answer every one.
> (Col. 4:5–6)

Gentiles. Crooked and perverse generation. Outsiders. All are designations of the real persons who have not yet received the light. The church is always to be aware of its behavior in the presence of these. The church is to be conscious that it is the gospel on display. It is to be a living demonstration of God's purpose for his new humanity. We, as Christians, really want the non-Christians (*Gentiles*, in New Testament usage) to look at us, to be intrigued by our new life, to watch us carefully to see if we're "for real." It is because we want them to "taste and see that the Lord is good" that we expose ourselves to the risks of opening our services to them.

This also explains why the letters to the churches say what they do. The general format for these letters is that they contain a doctrinal section, which is followed by a practical section. And the practical section is taken up with dealing with the relation of believers to one another, the mutual ministry, their appropriation of the new life in Christ. The practical sections do not deal with our relation to non-Christians explicitly, only by inference. But they do acknowledge that we are what we are, and live as we do, as those being watched by non-Christians.

We need to stop here and say it again. Many congregations are anti-evangelistic! Their inner lives as communities of the kingdom are so disreputable that any self-respecting pagan looking at them would be inclined to say: "If that is what the Christian faith produces, forget it!" This is part of the scandal of the church. When the world sees our quarrels, our loveless-ness, our unforgiving spirit, our complicity with unrighteous-ness, our gracelessness—then the world observes a denial of the gospel on the part of those who profess to believe it.

We should not be defensive about doing regular evaluations of our community life. Each congregation ought to ask itself what its communal life looks like to an outsider. Put yourself in the shoes of a stranger or a seeker and look at the life of your particular church. Ask yourself: What evidence would there be, what demonstration, of the joyous news of Jesus? What display would there be that God loves people like me? What would say to me that there is anything unique about you?

Or, live even more dangerously. Do a questionnaire and go out on a survey of the neighborhood in which your church house is located. This might be very revealing. Ask several questions such as:

1. Have you ever heard of the First Presbyterian Church?

2. Do you know any of its members?
3. Do you know where it meets?
4. What do you think it contributes to the neighborhood?
5. Do you have any idea what it stands for?
6. The people of First Church believe that God loves people like them and like you. Have they made this known in any way?

Unless these "Gentiles" in your community are architects or city planners, they probably won't have any acute interest in your church building. If the members park and block their driveways on Sunday morning, they might find your membership an offense. If they are musical, they might find your musical program interesting, or they might find it aesthetically obscene. The question is, what do your people look like to the non-Christian people around?

In the part of the country in which I live it is still respectable to belong to a church, or at least to give lip-service to it. There are multitudes of church buildings with signboards and newspaper displays. But a signboard or a newspaper display that says "Our Church Cares" is a cheap substitute for some real people who demonstrate that they do. Do you see the point? The gospel must be demonstrable; it must be on display in personal and interpersonal terms. That is the point that the New Testament epistles are making.

The Gallup Poll Organization and a number of Christian organizations and denominations recently did a survey on "The Unchurched American." It was a very illuminating bit of research. But it was also very frightening. For all of the attitudes of the unchurched American toward the church, one fact filtered through unmistakably. That fact was that the church has done a very poor job of communicating its Christian message to the people of this country. There are some 89 million people who are in the church. That is a sizable body of professing Christians. There are only 60 million who are unchurched, according to this survey. You would think that such a majority would have at least established the basis of its faith in Jesus the

Lord. Not so. The non-Christian, or unchurched, in this survey
seemed not to perceive anything having to do with Jesus or his
kingdom in the existence of the church. That is a devastating
observation.

Let's move on and see what ought to be manifest (evident)
in the Christian community. We know that all human beings
tend to share in three anxieties or concerns:

> 1. The anxiety over the transcendental *meaning* of life.
> What is life all about? Is there such a thing as truth that
> gives orientation?
>
> 2. The anxiety over *acceptance.* Does anyone care that
> I'm here? If there is a God, what does he think about me?
> Am I accepted, loved? If people knew all about me would
> they reject me? Would God?
>
> 3. The anxiety over *death.* Is death obliteration? Is there
> life after death? Am I accountable for my life? What's
> beyond the grave?

Now, we need to ask ourselves: What does the church have to
say to people who are struggling with these anxieties?

Faith, Hope, Love

We spoke earlier of the church being a community of faith,
hope, and love. Paul seems to have these three characteristics
of our Christian faith very much on his mind. In one way or
another they keep coming through in his writings, and well
they might. Because, looking at those anxieties above, we see an
unmistakable relation. Our Christian faith does in fact "scratch
where people itch."

Persons looking for the *meaning* of life, ought to find the
Christian community a place where life's most profound issues
are addressed in the light of Jesus Christ. The non-Christian
should see *faith* in our community. Our lives individually and
corporately should be oriented by our persuasion that God has
spoken personally and savingly in his Son.

The non-Christian ought to be brought face-to-face with the
question: What is your life all about? Jesus Christ spoke to that

question in his own teachings time and time again. Christians should not be afraid of the difficult questions of life. We are a community of truth where the transcendental meaning of life is experienced in Jesus Christ, and we should not sing that song pianissimo. Our commitment to the truth of the reality of the kingdom of God should be observable.

Persons looking for *acceptance,* likewise, ought to find the *love* of God demonstrated in the Christian community. And it should be demonstrated toward them. Persons are important to God. He came to seek and to save the lost, to call not the righteous but sinners to repentance. That kind of love is not always easy. Redemptive love is not unprincipled love. But the observable love of Christians for each other in the community is to be there for all to see. We love because God first loved us. Acceptance is upon the basis of grace, not merit. That grace also is on display.

And *hope?* How is that exhibited? We are a community that is on tiptoe with expectation. We are God's Easter people. The resurrection opens up all the options. *Death* loses its sting. The grave loses its victory. We are no longer in bondage to the fear of death. We are free. We are eagerly expecting what the Spirit of the risen Christ will do next among us and in history. This hope gives the Christian community its "zing." In the most despicable of circumstances, in the most overwhelming of crises, we have tasted the beginnings of kingdom life by the Holy Spirit, and we are in anticipation of its consummation. And so we sing and give praise to God.

Kingdom Values, Signs and Wonders

The experience in the community of the kingdom of God gives us a whole unique set of values. One only has to read the Sermon on the Mount to see the social, economic, political, and ethical values that come from being God's holy people. Perhaps there is no more graphic witness in the world than in those areas where our light shines in the greatest contrast to the darkness around us. Issues like how we spend our money, how we value our family life, how we deal with human need, how we view human sexuality, how we resolve differences, how we forgive our enemies—these are all areas where our kingdom behavior exhibits itself in sharp contrast to the distorted values of this age. If non-Christians look and see us doing as much as praying about these matters, then they know that there is something at work in us that sets us apart.

The New Testament speaks also of signs and wonders. I believe that God still performs such things as miracles when and where he pleases. But in the ordinary life of a congregation there are always the signs and wonders of changed lives and of answered prayers. Nothing is so evangelizing in a congregation as a life transformed by the power of God. Nothing causes the mundane to give way to excitement as when, in the face of a humanly impossible situation, God intervenes in answer to his people's prayer and brings a solution. And don't think that these things are not watched by our "Gentile" friends!

One splendid Christian spokesman made the comment that the early church evangelized by preaching the gospel, by singing the gospel, by arguing it and acting it out in drama—but primarily it evangelized the ancient world by its breathless excitement. That breathless excitement is the component of our communal life that communicates nonverbally to our non-Christian observers.

Dear friends, we are the body of Christ. We are in the world that the world may see the glory of God in the church. Before we talk of further efforts in the work of evangelization, we need to be before God on our faces to enlist his help with that work in us by the Holy Spirit that will make the congregation to which we belong to be the gospel on display!

Disciplemaking

A logical question at this point is: How do you begin to develop a congregation that is the gospel on display? Well, to start with, we need to begin to take seriously the biblical discipline of disciplemaking. The Great Commission in Matthew's

Gospel doesn't talk in general terms about preaching the gospel around the world. No, it says that we are to "make disciples" and to teach them to observe everything that Christ has commanded. Now that involves a lot more than just preaching!

A good beginning place is a new member development plan for your congregation. A significant part of our problem is that we get Christians "birthed" and baptized into the church and then assume that they have an understanding of kingdom life. Disciplemaking, which is a particular Greek word used in Matthew, has to do with not only instructing a person in the truth but also demonstrating it, spending time with that person in a refining process until he or she learns how to live the truth.

Every congregation I know of that is displaying the gospel is a congregation where every person coming into that congregation spends time with a person or a team of persons who are mature and who assist them into the new life of the people of God by instruction and by demonstration. In some Christian communities this process is more formal; in others it is quite informal. But young Christians and new members need to know what is involved in being the children of the heavenly Father. This is particularly true (believe it or not) where persons who are already professing Christians come from another congregation where the gospel is *anything but* displayed. Such persons have learned a style of behavior that is antithetical to the gospel, and so when they come into your congregation they have to be both "untaught" and "taught," lest they become problem children in the community.

This book you are reading could be a guide to new member development. Most congregations work out their own new member equipping course and continually refine it, change it, and keep it flexible enough to compensate for particular circumstances. This requires some mature and attractive Christian persons who are committed to new member equipping as their major ministry. It may be the pastor in a small church, or the elders. In larger congregations that I have observed, it is a team for whom this is their primary ministry in the congregation.

Disciplemaking takes time, both in groups and one-on-one. But it is not fair to receive a person into the community of faith and not spend the time with that person that will provide him or her with the resources for living out the gospel.

Here is the outline of the most recent new member course that I have done (I change it regularly). You will see in it the flavor of our congregation and of this course. It is designed to be a seven week course. Members are given copies of a brief history of the congregation, of our membership covenant, and of our denominational tradition. The seven topics are as follows:

    I.   A Community of Faith

    II.   A Community of Freedom

    III.   A Community of Christian Growth

    IV.   You and the Community in a World of Darkness

    V.   A Community of Evangelism

    VI.   You, the Body of Christ, and Your Gifts

    VII.   A Community with Oversight and Authority

You may ask: Why these particular topics out of all the possible things a new member might need to know? These emerged out of our congregational life. Certain events and stresses brought our team of elders to believe that these topics were significant. But such a course is just a beginning. It takes discussion and quality time spent with the new members to enable them to function maturely in the community.

So, settle it in your minds as a Christian community and as Christian persons: we as the people of the kingdom of God are on display. When people want to know what God is all about, what the Christian faith is all about, what the kingdom of God is all about, they have a right to look at us and observe the answer. Our aim is to demonstrate "what is the will of God, what is good and acceptable and perfect" (Rom. 12:2).

What a calling! What a challenge! What a gospel!

Now on to another dimension of our witness.

CHAPTER 13
The Witness of
the Worshiping Community

The Christian community being the community of the kingdom, when that community gathers together to worship its glorious God and King, it is giving witness to its faith. The joyous news of the kingdom is being celebrated. The congregation is being evangelized afresh with the wonder of what God has done in his Son, Jesus Christ.

But listen! Something else happens. Many, if not most, non-Christians who are curious about the claims of the Christian faith will seek out the church when it gathers for worship to observe, to listen, and to evaluate. This is especially true if they have no close Christian friend with whom to talk. Visitors who turn up at the church's worship times are frequently inquirers into the faith. The more vigorous a Christian community is, the more this will be true. There are many "shoppers," people who want to see what kind of wares the Christian church is offering. Many of these are not at the point of even wanting to talk about it. They do not want to be pressured into "joining" the church. But there they are. They have taken the initiative to come into a Christian family gathering. They have taken, if you will, a certain risk. So the ordinary worship services of the Christian community have an unmistakable evangelizing dimension that must never be overlooked.

Let me be the first to disclaim that the *primary* purpose of a Sunday morning worship service is evangelistic. Some Christian groups believe that. I do not. Our primary purpose in such services is the worship of our God, who is worthy to be worshiped. But that does not mean that we overlook the evangelistic dimension and potential of such times. It will be worth our while to take time here then to reflect on the possibilities of such worship times, and not only the regular weekly worship services of the community, but also those other times in the life of the church and in the liturgical year that have evangelistic possibilities.

Weekly Gathering for Worship

Put yourself into the place of an inquirer who is a stranger to the life and customs of the Christian community. I can well remember the first time I, an avowed Protestant, visited a Roman Catholic Church to see what that Christian tradition was all about. I was, first off, a bit frightened, because I had always heard that there was ill feeling between Catholics and Protestants. I felt that I was an intruder. Then I was a stranger to the liturgy. It seemed that about the time I was getting up, everybody else was kneeling again. I couldn't find my place in anything, and was always a straggler in the responses. Everyone else seemed to be thoroughly at home with what they were doing, and I felt that every eye was looking at me suspiciously. There was nothing to make me feel the least bit oriented, accepted, or welcomed there. It wasn't until years later when a Catholic community ministered to me that I got over that feeling of estrangement.

This illustrates, though, some of the emotions that are present in our non-Christian friends who gird up their misgivings and step over the threshold into our church house on a Sunday morning. What can we do to share our joy and love in Christ Jesus with such persons?

Greeters and Ushers

I really believe that those volunteers who greet people at the door and assist them to their seats are a very significant group. I am acquainted with congregations where the ushers and greeters look upon this as their major ministry in the body. They gather early for prayer that God, by his Spirit, will make them alert and sensitive to every person who enters the sanctuary for worship. This is especially true for those who are troubled, or who are visitors. It is a marvelous token of our caring if someone takes time to find out visitors' names, to be available to answer any questions, to show them the order of worship, to seat them, and, if possible, to introduce them to members who can sit with them and explain what is going on. Such ushers can often get visitors' names and addresses, and put into their hands an explanatory piece of literature. But just to be acknowledged as real persons who are appreciated and welcomed is a beautiful start.

Explanation

I was never taught that explanation was an integral part of the worship service, but now I think that it helps Christians and non-Christians alike as they come to a service of worship. As a matter of fact, I learned the technique from a radio preacher of some renown. His congregation broadcasted its service from a large city, and I had heard many controversial things about his theology. Yet, on one Sunday morning when I was ill, I listened. I don't remember much about his sermon, but I remember that he spent the first couple of minutes acquainting the congregation with why they were there and what would be taking place in the next hour together. Though only a radio listener, I felt as if I knew what would be transpiring—what he said tied the whole service together.

I have used this plan over the years to great profit. In our church the choir ordinarily sang a call to worship. Because we were not a large church, I could go in on the congregational level and, standing on that floor level in front of the first pew, I would (after the greeting) take a moment to explain who we were, why we were there, and what would be the thrust of our worship, hymns, scripture, and message on that day. In so doing I had in mind especially those who might not know what a Christian community was all about. But in saying who we were I was declaring the fact that we were there because of Jesus Christ, who loved us and had called us to be his people.

Frequently I would use a paraphrase of some scriptural passage, and this had an evangelizing effect. Take, for instance:

> "Brothers and sisters, it is the Lord's day. We are here because Jesus Christ has loved us and loosed us from our sins by his blood and made us a kingdom, priests to his God and Father. To him be glory and dominion forever and ever. Amen. As we worship him today, our theme will be . . ."

That scripture is from Revelation, chapter one. It says something of our self-awareness as Christ's people. Another would be a similar paraphrase from 1 John 1:

> "Brothers and sisters, we are here because we have experienced Jesus Christ. We have known him and proclaim the eternal life which was with the Father and has been made known to us. We are here to proclaim him and to share in the fellowship which we have with the Father and with his Son Jesus Christ. In the moments before us we are going to be rejoicing in his promise, etc. . . ."

A brief survey of the hymns and the lesson from scripture, then, gives the whole congregation a renewed sense of what this hour together is all about. It clues in the stranger as to the identity of the congregation.

Greeting

Right there with the explanation is a good place for a greeting. Many congregations which I have visited wait until the service is half over to greet the congregation. I like to see it done at the outset. Either before or right after the explanation, the congregation should be welcomed in the name of Jesus Christ. It's like the host standing at the door of a home and welcoming in the guests. And it offers an opportunity in a nonthreatening way to acknowledge the visitors. There are many ways to do this, but I would say something like this:

> "Some of you are here for the first time. We are delighted you are here. A special welcome to you. We do not want you to feel a stranger. We want you to know the love of

God in Christ as we do. Thank you for coming to be with us today."

In our church I invited the congregation at that point to turn and greet each other so that no one would be alone or a stranger. This caused several minutes of bedlam but it was worth it. (Even if the leader of worship—the pastor or whoever—doesn't do this, it would be a valuable tradition to encourage your resident membership to be alert to those around them and to welcome visitors.)

Call to Worship

Last Sunday I visited a congregation where the call to worship had an evangelistic note. The pastor called the congregation to worship with the passage:

> "Come to me, all who labor and are heavy laden, and I will give you rest. Take my yoke upon you, and learn from me; for I am gentle and lowly in heart, and you will find rest for your souls. For my yoke is easy, and my burden is light."   (Matt. 11:28–30)

Having said that, he added: "This is the invitation of Jesus Christ to you. Keep that in mind as we worship him today." With that, the organ sounded the chord for a hymn of praise and we were off. But that call to worship was an offering of the invitation of Christ to those who were present.

Confession and Absolution

There is a threadbare story told in church circles about the two gentlemen who had celebrated a bit too robustly and intemperately on Saturday night. On the Sunday morning after they were feeling the effects of their indulgence with some remorse and decided that perhaps it would help if they would go to church. As the story goes, they made their way warily up to the Baptist church and heard the strains of "Blessed Assurance, Jesus Is Mine" coming forth, and they didn't feel too comfortable with that. So they tried again at the Presbyterian church, but again the hymn, "I Sing the Mighty Power of God," was a little more than their guilty souls could bear. But they got to the Episcopal church just as the congregation was praying the prayer of confession:

> ". . . We have erred, and strayed from thy ways like lost sheep. We have followed too much the devices and desires of our own hearts. We have offended against thy holy laws. We have left undone those things which we ought to have done; And we have done those things which we ought not to have done; And there is no health in us. . . ."

At that point one of the gentlemen looked at the other through bleary eyes and said: "That's our kind of folks. Let's go in!"

It is true that our first confession as Christians is that we are all sinners. And we don't stop being sinners when we become Christians. John warns that when we say we are without sin we are only deceiving ourselves (1 John 1:8). It is of the essence of our good news that God loves sinners, and that's us. To a troubled person in our congregation, it is enormously encouraging to find out that there is mercy with the Lord.

In my own Reformed tradition our father in the faith John Calvin felt that the high point in the worship service was at the point after the prayers of confession when the minister declared forgiveness to all who truly repented and trusted in Jesus Christ. To Calvin that was the moment when the gospel was declared in all of its beauty.

The prayer of confession in a worship service is needed by the believing congregation. But it may also be to the point to acknowledge that the prayer is needed by some in the congregation because they have never accepted God's redeeming love in Jesus Christ.

The declaration of forgiveness gives the leader of worship all kinds of opportunity to state the gospel again: John 3:16; Luke 19:10; 1 John 1:9–10; Romans 8:1. Christians need to hear these promises over and over again. But imagine the effect on a non-Christian sitting in your assembly who has always thought that one had to get it all together and be perfect before one could be a Christian. Or think what it would be like to assume that God had long ago written you off as an incorrigible scoundrel, then to hear that God sent his Son to seek and to save people just like you! So the confession and absolution are an evangelizing moment.

The Prayers

One sadly confesses that some of the prayers one hears in worship services can be very narcissistic, while others can be so dispassionate that one might as well be reading a telephone directory. Prayers should be that point where the congregation offers up its concerns not only for itself but for the community and the world to God the Father. The prayers of a congregation say a great deal about the faith and perspective of the people of God. It is in prayer, perhaps more than anywhere else, that the compassion of the Lord flows through his people. It is in the prayers that they present themselves as a pilgrim people to their heavenly Father on behalf of this world in darkness.

It doesn't take much imagination to realize that an inquirer would learn a great deal about the love of God and the purpose of God in listening to such prayers.

Think also of how much a congregation can be made alert to its responsibility to the world through the prayers of the morning worship. Issues of justice, human need, the plight of the victims of tragedies, and the lostness of those outside of Christ can be lifted to God in prayer. If a congregation is evangelistically insensitive, then the prayers of the congregation, the pastoral prayer, are a good place to begin preparation. The whited harvest field is all around us, and the prayers of supplication and intercession need to include this world that God so loved!

The Offering

Would you believe the offering is a place for evangelization? I stumbled into this realization quite by accident (a significant portion of my Christian growth happens this way). I kept hearing the comments by outsiders that every time they came to church they were asked for money. I could appreciate their response. After all, why should they put money in the offering plate? They didn't belong to this outfit! If they weren't even sure what they thought of God, or if there is one, why should they part with their hard-earned cash? Yet the whole thing disturbed me. The question we have to ask ourselves is: What does our Lord want of these persons? What does he expect of them and what does he want to do for them?

So, quite on impulse one Sunday morning at the time of the offering of gifts to the Lord, I made a statement, something like this, which has become almost liturgical with me:

> "The bringing of tithes and offerings to the Lord is the privilege of those who have received him as Savior and as Lord. We bring him our tithes in token of our trust that he is the giver of every good and perfect gift. We bring him offerings above our tithes in response to his extravagant and overflowing love to us. If you have never received him as Savior and Lord, what the Lord wants from you is not your money, but your heart, your trust in him. And he wants to give you eternal life. Let us worship God with our morning tithes and offerings."

That lets everybody know just what we're doing, Christian and non-Christian alike. When I first did this, my deacons almost choked! They thought I was discouraging a money source. Interestingly enough (I am not establishing this as a spiritual axiom), from the time I instituted that explanation, the giving of our congregation increased! I think one thing that happened was that it waked up a lot of sleepy and uncertain church members to the dynamic of our faith and called forth some healthy soul searching.

Announcements

I am one pastor who despises announcements and makes as few as possible. After all, we go to the trouble to print an order of worship with congregational announcements on it, so why should I redundantly go over them again? But there is always something important to be announced, so we have a slot in the worship service to do it. In that moment many congregations, like ours, have a tradition that everybody signs a pad and passes it down the row of seats for others to do the same. We call it the "Ritual of Friendship." As the pad passes back down to its origin, folks can see who else is there.

Since each Sunday I have to encourage the worshipers to sign the friendship pad, it does make for an appropriate time to say a word to those who are visitors. Again we express our joy at their presence. But also it gives an occasion to say again what we are about as the people of Jesus Christ. Rather than putting pressure on them to "accept Christ" or to "join the church," I offer a sincere but gentle invitation to them:

> "If you are here with us and have never considered the claims of Jesus Christ, who he is, what he promises, then we would like more than anything to be able to share with you the wonderful news of God's love for you in Jesus Christ. At your convenience we will sit down with you and answer your questions about what it means to belong to Christ. All you need do is make this known to us. And if you are already a Christian but not a member of a local church we would like to invite you to consider what it means to be a part of this congregation. Christians need to belong to a congregation of God's people, and if this congregation is not to your liking, we will be happy to put you in contact with one that is. God bless you!"

That takes all of forty-five seconds and is well worth it. We keep well-chosen and brief pieces of literature to put into people's hands. We are ready to have someone sit down with them on the spot after the service. The pastors also are ready to schedule appointments.

Parenthetically, the follow-up on the "Ritual of Friendship" includes a letter that goes out on Monday morning and says something of the same thing. It expresses our joy that the visitors have been with us. Then it explains what a Christian community is and the basis of membership through faith in Jesus as Savior and Lord. We leave no misunderstanding of our character as God's family, and then we make ourselves available to discuss that with our visitors at their request. There is a response card in the letter. Usually a telephone contact is made about a week later, with no pressure, just a personal word of greeting and the invitation to visitors to avail themselves of the opportunities of the congregation.

The Sermon

Different congregations and different pastors have different styles of preaching. But you can count on it, the visitors who come into your congregation will be listening to see if the message out of the pulpit relates to the real world and the real life which are theirs. If one is faithfully preaching from the scriptures, then there is going to have to be, of necessity, a relation of any text to that consummation of revelation which is Jesus Christ. In that sense there is an inescapable evangelistic element in every sermon. The patriarch may be speaking to Israel as God's chosen people; the psalmist may be dealing with anger at the enemies of God; the prophet may be chastising the people of Judah for forgetting who they are; or Mark may be speaking of Jesus, who came not to call the righteous but sinners to repentance. Whatever the text, it is all part of that revelation of God's redemptive purpose which consummates in Jesus Christ. That focus must be kept clear. The purpose of the sermon at the worship service is primarily for the instruction and edification of the worshipers, but it must not overlook that unevangelized visitor who is there listening to hear whether there is good news!

One wise old Christian teacher instructed young preachers to include enough of Christ in every sermon so that if someone were there who had never heard the gospel before and left never to hear it again that person would have heard enough to be saved. Good advice!

Are gospel invitations appropriate in worship services? I raise the question only because so many feel that unless a "gospel invitation" is extended so that people may physically respond evangelism has not been done thoroughly. The answer to this question depends a great deal on the tradition of the congregation. There is nothing illegitimate about asking people to respond to Christ by standing or coming forward, though in the context of a worship service it would seem that this would be the exception rather than the rule. If the scripture lesson and sermon of the morning lay down a strong challenge to a response of faith, the sermon might well be concluded with the challenge to act upon God's convicting word. Each Christian congregation or tradition will have its own way of making that challenge explicit. The important thing is that the demands of the gospel should never be muted or made a casual option in the community of faith.

As the scriptures are faithfully preached there will be an evangelizing effect. My own tradition and style, coming from our Calvinistic heritage, is to preach consecutive expository sermons. This means that I preach right through a book of the Bible consecutively. This is also called *didactic* preaching, or *teaching* preaching. In doing this we are equipping the congregation to be biblically literate and consequently ever more thoroughly evangelized and excited about the Christian message. The congregational results of this type of preaching are most heartening.

Implementation

I am aware that I have been writing here like a preacher. What if you are not a preacher? Where are the handles for you in seeing the evangelistic potential of the weekly gathering for worship realized? If you are not the one who is responsible for worship, what then?

I don't think any layperson ought to take lightly the responsibility he or she has to influence what goes on in the worship time. A pastor who is not sensitive to what the Holy Spirit might be saying through the congregation needs to be talked to. The service of worship does not belong to the pastor. The pastor is not infallible. The congregation ought to find a time periodically to sit down and talk and pray about the worship service with the pastor or priest.

The members of our congregation asked our elders if we could have once each quarter a Sunday morning service that was explicitly evangelistic, to which they would be encouraged to bring their non-Christian friends. Our elders responded favorably to this request. Now, on the designated Sundays, we include testimonies or witnesses by laypersons of their faith in Christ. The music is chosen carefully. The whole atmosphere is a bit more informal, and the sermon is a direct presentation of the life and claims of Jesus Christ as the only Savior and Lord. Sometimes laypersons do the preaching, since they are often better evangelists than are the clergy-types.

But such services are the exception. It is the faithful witness of the gospel of the kingdom every time the congregation gathers for worship that should be our norm, and the congregation and pastor are a team in this ministry.

Special Celebrations

A word needs to be said about the evangelizing effect of the other special celebrations that are common to our kingdom communities.

Baptisms. What a marvelous occasion to speak of the entrance into kingdom life, the new life in Christ. Baptism is the sacrament of entrance into the Christian community and into the communion of the Holy Spirit. One only need look at the baptismal formula in the previous section of this book to realize how pregnant with meaning is this visual aid to the gospel. All the symbolism of the washing of regeneration, the dying with Christ and the resurrection to newness of life, the forsaking of darkness and the entering into light, and even the gospel promises to parents on behalf of their children are graphically enacted in the sacrament of baptism.

It is not at all inappropriate in adult baptisms to have the candidates for baptism give a brief word of witness about how Christ has worked in their lives to bring them to that moment. The moment is so fraught with drama that the pastor could suggest by way of invitation that there might be others in the congregation who have not yet come to Christ who might want to make this a moment of moral and spiritual decision. When people see their friends making such life-changing decisions, it has a powerful effect on their own spiritual inertia.

The Lord's Supper. There it is, right out in front of the congregation. The gospel that can be seen, touched, tasted, and ingested. The body and blood of Christ. The words of institution. The gospel of sins forgiven rehearsed. The focus on the cross and the atoning death of Christ for us. There are so many ways this can be used to reevangelize a congregation that it is sobering that the Lord's Supper could ever become routine. I really believe that the Lord Jesus gave us this sacrament as an instrument of revival in the truest sense of that term.

The invitation to that table has two sides to it. On the one hand, the church invites all who truly repent and believe to come, no matter how unworthy they may feel. On the other hand, the church warns those who are unrepentant, harboring rebellion and sin, or at odds with a fellow, not to come, at least not until they have come clean with God and their neighbor. The church also asks the unbaptized not to come. Paul says that to come unworthily is spiritually hazardous because the person coming carelessly doesn't discern the body of Christ (the church).

I, for one, have seen unbelievers come to Christ in the presence of that sacrament. But more, I have seen careless church members come to life-changing new faith in the presence of the bread and wine. It is an awesome and joyous moment, the high point of all Christian worship. And the Holy Spirit witnesses through that sacrament in a most unique way. It is an exclusive moment. It is for believers only. It is the one time the Christian church excludes those who are outside the household of faith. But even this exclusion can be done with such compassion that the outsider will be constrained to consider the message of Christ.

Never underestimate the evangelizing impact of the sacrament of holy communion.

Funerals. More non-Christian friends turn up in the church house for a funeral than for almost any other occasion. Friends come to "pay their respects" to the deceased. And what do the Christians do? They celebrate Easter, the resurrection of the dead through Christ Jesus. Non-Christians come with their anxiety over death, and Christians say: "The Lord is risen. O death where is thy sting? O grave where is thy victory?" Funerals are a time of worship when the great moment of our Christian faith is joyously heralded: we are free from the fear of death because of the resurrection of Jesus Christ from the dead. We sing the Easter hymns. We affirm our faith in God "our help in ages past, our hope for years to come."

A Christian funeral can boggle the minds of non-Christian friends and can set them on a pilgrimage at the end of which is Christ. Hallelujah!

Weddings. Another service of worship for which non-Christian friends show up is a wedding. Now granted, a lot of weddings are also a lot of sentimental schmaltz. But a wedding happens when two particular persons and the congregation of the household of faith come before God to testify to the sanctity of marriage and the family. It is a time of hearing scripture and of taking vows that constitute a new family. It is a time of hearing afresh of God's purpose in maleness and femaleness and marriage.

Consider, if you will, in a generation where marriage and family crises have reached epidemic proportions, what a significant moment a wedding is for the family of the Lord's people. Every person who is in that service as a guest hears anew the word of God having to do with the responsibilities of husbands and wives. The gospel of the kingdom brings marriage and family under the Lordship of Jesus Christ and reestablishes their sanctity. The witness of the Christian conception of marriage is in no small way a powerful agent of evangelism. Marriages and families are hurting in this present dominion of darkness, and God comes bringing light and meaning and power—a whole new creation involving marriage and the family.

The Liturgical Year

We Christians, God's kingdom people, have our family traditions. Often the secular society piggybacks on this and makes them a merchandising heyday. But that shouldn't hinder us from claiming them as ours and using them for all they're worth. It doesn't really matter that they have been confused with ancient pagan festivals. With a bit of boldness and imagination we can use them as moments of proclamation.

Advent. The celebration of the long-awaited coming of God into human history.

Christmas. The celebration of the incarnation of God into human form at the birth of Jesus Christ. The Messiah is come.

Epiphany. Did you ever stop to think that there is no feast day for missionary purposes in the liturgical year? It is because this theme is celebrated in Epiphany, when we remember how the Gentiles came to worship at the crib of Jesus. Epiphany is our missionary season, and speaks of God's redeeming love for those "outside."

Lent. A time of sober reflection on how seriously God takes our sin and rebellion, so much so that he gave his Son. Our clear explanation of this to our non-Christian friends is necessary in evangelization.

Easter. By his death Jesus absorbed all the rebellion of humanity and the wrath of God against sin. But Easter is the triumph of God over death and hell and the exaltation of Christ as Lord over all. All of his claims and promises are substantiated in his resurrection. Easter is one "hallelujah day" and we need to use it for all it's worth.

Pentecost. Pentecost is an often overlooked feast day in the Christian community, and this to our detriment. This is the celebration of the coming of the Spirit of God to indwell and empower the church. That's exciting! That human beings are indwelt by God himself so that the resurrection power of Christ is available to us is no small good news!

We might turn a few heads if we sent all of our friends well-composed and artistically done greeting cards at Epiphany or Pentecost rather than Christmas. While they weren't looking, we could feed them some of the wonders of God's unimaginable love and the heritage of the Christian community. Wouldn't that be fun?

Extraordinary Events

A final word on certain occasions that bring the community of the King before the watching world so that the depth of our faith shines through: I'm thinking of the Christian community coping with crises. Our non-Christian friends will be curious as to how we handle those tragic times, those deeps of human agony. I'm thinking of one illustration out of our congregational life. One of our greatly loved families had been off for a weekend together and was returning. The parents were in one car and the three children in another. In a collision all three children were killed instantly. The congregation was called together that night for prayer because all were caught up in the sorrow, the questions, the inexplicable ways of God's providence.

It was a tearful night, though not without hope. But the parents sent word asking that the congregation pray for the drunken man who had caused the accident and who was not seriously hurt. There was at least one person who had come to that prayer service out of curiosity, and that evening was a turning point. The amazing power of Jesus Christ in human lives was evident in the midst of the tragic. That's evangelism also.

We have seen people convicted and converted during days of prayer and fasting, and at prayer meetings that were designed for anything but evangelism. I recall one prayer meeting of some university students who had gathered to confess to God what a botch they had made of an evangelistic effort and to pray over their failure to reach their friends with the gospel. One friend didn't have any better sense than to follow her Christian friend from supper up to the prayer gathering. And in listening to the Christians pour out their hearts to God she was convinced of her need of Christ and became a believer. As that semester went on, the prayer meeting became the scene of several remarkable conversions.

I have gone to some length to make the point that our life as God's worshiping people is of evangelistic significance beyond all imagining. All we need to do is to be sensitive to this fact and to ask God by his own life-giving Spirit to so make us alive with the joyous news of the kingdom of God that anyone who gets close will be infected with our gospel.

CHAPTER 14
Sheer Enthusiasm, Devotion to Christ, and Ready Conversation

Our generation is one of "psycho-babble," endless psychological table talk, usually by people who have very little idea what they are talking about. We diagnose ourselves and each other ad nauseam. One diagnosis that is common among us is that such and such a person has an "identity crisis." By this we mean that a person doesn't really know who he or she is, which makes the person's character, how to say it, a bit fluid.

I raise this point only by way of asserting in the strongest possible terms that those of us who belong to Jesus Christ, who are his kingdom people, must not have an identity crisis. There *are* many mysteries in this life. There are many things we do not know, mysteries which we share with the rest of humanity. But who God is, how he has spoken in Christ, that he has bidden us come into his new order through repentance and faith, and that he has brought light into the darkness—about all this we are quite certain, even dogmatic. We people of the kingdom do not operate on fragile assumptions or vain hopes but on the word of our King, who is Lord of all. Jesus Christ is the sure foundation of our Christian church and of our Christian faith.

This certainty is our heritage from the Father. The joyous news of the kingdom of God, the gospel of God's Son, is our very lifeblood and the source of our breathless excitement. You find those Christians after Pentecost rehearsing the data together, praying over it, discussing it, sharing it in their lives and over the dinner table.

That this may not be true in many Christian lives and congregations simply signals the need for such lives and congregations to be reevangelized. When Christians are ill at ease in
discussing the faith, then something is badly amiss. Such folks
need to rub against some Christians who are alive and excited.
They need a disciplemaker, someone who can help them into
a simple but articulate confidence in discussing the faith they
have in Jesus Christ. This is where Christian conferences can be
of help. To be with other excited Christians can be heartening.
In recent times, "Lay Witness" missions have been useful, as
bands of fresh and articulate Christians have come into congregations to share their lives and their faith in Jesus Christ. Home
Bible studies have been helpful in drawing Christians together
in informal home settings to discuss scripture, making it easier
for them to cough up questions and to iron out difficulties that
have been stumbling blocks.

Some Christians are shy and some are gregarious. Some are
people with quick and perceptive minds, while others are a bit
slower. Yet all Christians need to be free to discuss their lives
in Jesus Christ with other Christians, or with non-Christians.
Such news as that which we have in Jesus Christ cannot morally
be kept to ourselves.

Do you remember the account of the four lepers who went
to the camp of the Syrians (2 Kings 7) at the time when Ben-
hadad's army had besieged Samaria to the point of famine?
When they came into the camp they found that it was empty.
The Syrians had fled because of one of God's startling interven-
tions. There was all that food and provision. They began to loot
it, and then had second thoughts: "We are not doing right. This
day is a day of good news; . . . let us go and tell the king's
household" (2 Kings 7:9). So with us. It is a day of good news.
It is no "ho-hum" thing that God has done. We must not be
silent about it. Some will insist that they will simply witness by
their lives. Well and good, but as someone has put it: Word
without life is hypocrisy, but life without word is mystery! We
Christians cannot but speak of what we have seen and heard.

It is also quite common to try and defer to those others who are the "evangelists" for the church. Yes, there is such a person as an evangelist. This is one of the gifts of the Holy Spirit. Every congregation ought to be on the lookout for those who have this gift within their company. The gift of evangelism is not easy to put your finger on in the Bible, but references to it seem to speak of those who really have a capacity for speaking the gospel to non-Christians and who love to do it. They are good at "mixing it up" with those who are strangers to the faith and getting a hearing. My hunch is that these are probably going to be laypersons in today's church. Sometimes they are the musicians who put the gospel into music and sing it, and so get a hearing. But evangelists are only going to be a small percentage of any Christian congregation.

The Work Is Done by Ordinary Christians

Listen! We've learned a lot about evangelism in recent years. We've had the big evangelistic crusades, and the evangelistic superstars. Praise God for them. They've been useful in many ways. But they aren't the ones who bring the masses of the people to Christ. Did you know that? People may watch these persons on television, but they can't really relate to that shining figure preaching to forty thousand people. No, studies in church growth have shown that something over seventy percent of all the people who come to Christ and into the church come because *a close friend or a relative* shares Christ with them and invites them into the faith and into the church. It is somebody they know very well. It is the ordinary Christians who carry the burden of evangelism.

The popular evangelists may serve to sow the seeds of the gospel, or to get the message out there and begin the work in people's hearts and minds, but the real work is primarily done by "us folks" who are part of the Father's family in Christ Jesus. As we are on display before our friends every day, in the home, in the school, on the production line, in the office, on the route, in the hospital, or wherever, we need to prayerfully anticipate that they may be wondering what makes us tick.

These non-Christian friends have a right to be curious about us. We actually want them to be. They may also be a bit hostile. The convicting grace of God sometimes causes people to get hostile and defensive—even nasty—in the presence of our Christian character. But they should not be able to ignore us. With consummate grace and gentleness and love we ought to be ready to receive their challenges and their questions.

This is the gist of one of the clearest teachings about Christian witness in the New Testament. You will find it in 1 Peter 3:13–16 (J.B. Phillips, *The New Testament in Modern English*):

> After all, who in the ordinary way is likely to injure you for being enthusiastic for good? And if it should happen that you suffer "for righteousness' sake," that is a privilege. You need neither fear their threats nor worry about them; simply concentrate on being completely devoted to Christ in your hearts. Be ready at any time to give a quiet and reverent answer to any man who wants a reason for the hope that you have within you. Make sure that your conscience is perfectly clear, so that if men should speak slanderously of you as rogues they may come to feel ashamed of themselves for libeling your good Christian behavior.

Isn't that beautiful? It comes shortly after the passage which encourages us to maintain good conduct among the Gentiles (nonbelievers) so that they may see our good deeds and glorify God when they stand before him.

It is very interesting to me that there isn't any emphasis in the New Testament on assaulting other persons with the gospel. Such has been developed into a fine art by some under the name of evangelism. Mind you, I don't think that a deliberate and authoritative presentation of the gospel is at all illegitimate, *if* it is done with sensitivity to the other human being. But what I'm saying is that, as you search the New Testament to see how we communicate the light out into the darkness, you find passages like the one above. Our *holy lives* generate curiosity and questions among our non-Christian acquaintances, the people who know us and watch us. Peter, then, gives a very simple rule of thumb for our response:

1. *Be completely devoted to Christ in your hearts.* There should be no question in our hearts that we have responded to God's love in Christ and joyfully yielded up our lives to him so that he may possess us and remake us as his new humanity, his kingdom people. "Devoted to Christ"—that should be the mark of our lives.

2. *Be ready to give a quiet and reverent answer.* We should not obscure this opportunity with false humility, or foot-shuffling modesty. When people ask us why we have hope in Christ, they deserve a thoughtful answer given quietly, sensitively, and with reverence to God who is the object of our devotion. Our friends have a right to expect this of us. It may be as simple and amazed as the answer of the blind man to whom Jesus gave sight: "This I know—once I was blind, but now I see."

3. *Keep your conscience clear.* In the throes of spiritual struggle our non-Christian friends will be looking for any excuse to escape the moral confrontation with Christ. They will rejoice in flaws in your character. Peter says to keep your holy life right out there with a clear conscience, so if people want to bad-mouth you that's their problem and not yours.

People ought to be able to take us seriously as Christians. Beyond our excitement and our words there ought to be substance. And that very substance ought to evoke more questions.

Ready Conversation

Sam Shoemaker once commented that he wanted to make Pittsburgh as famous for God as it is for steel. I'd like to see Christians as ready to enter into conversation about Jesus Christ as they are about football, the weather, or organic gardening. By that I don't mean that Christians should be so one-tracked in their minds that they can't carry on a civil conversation about anything else. Christians ought to have ideas to rub one against another. They ought to be people who are alert to what is going on around them. But they ought also to be ready to discuss their faith and how it relates to a whole range of subjects.

Michael Green, in his Lausanne address, speaks of how questions are a superb way to get things moving in a conversation. Questions such as:

What is the point of living?
What is freedom and how do you get it?
Is violence inescapable?
What does it mean to be human?
What is the meaning of love?

All these questions, he says, lead straight to Jesus.[5]

Another Englishman who had a zeal to make Christ known was Prime Minister William Wilberforce. Wilberforce was one of a number of politicians, or government figures, in the last century known as the "Clapham Sect." They lived out of London in a rather well-to-do settlement known as Clapham. They were all good Anglican churchmen of evangelical persuasion. They spent a good deal of time talking and praying together as to how they could influence the course of the government for Christ. Wilberforce had a series of what he called "launchers." These were questions or statements calculated to provoke a conversation in which he could naturally share his conviction of the joyous news of Jesus Christ. He and his friends were remarkably successful in influencing parliament and their friends for Christ. We need to cultivate this art of Christian conversation. People who are our friends may not at every moment want to discuss spiritual things with us, but we should be ready when they do.

The place to cultivate this is to take such questions as Michael Green suggested above and discuss them in your church school class, or over the dinner table in your home. We learn significant conversation in the Christian fellowship, and refine it there, so that we are more comfortable with it when we are with our non-Christian friends.

Listening

A Christian who cannot listen will never be much good in sensitive conversation. Christians have too frequently come at others with memorized presentations and have missed the whole point of knowing what is going on in the life of the other person. Non-Christians are real human beings with feelings and questions. We do well to tune into their lives. The issues and questions that are on their minds will usually emerge in short order.

Your Story

We don't always have to wait for someone to ask us about our faith. With persons we know well, or persons who have come to us with questions, we have a right to let them know who we are. After all, we aren't neutral persons any more. We are persons in Christ.

It is entirely appropriate for us to say to friends something like this: "Harriet, we've been friends for a good while and I've never even shared with you the most thrilling discovery of my life. Have you got a minute for me to tell you about how I met Jesus Christ?" About ninety-five percent of the time our friends will be interested, but you've given them an out if they don't want to hear.

This can be done over coffee, in the car on a trip, or on any occasion where you have a few moments of free time for conversation. An exercise that every one of us ought to do regularly is as follows:

> For the moment imagine that your very best friend, whom you love and for whom you've prayed, is not a Christian. This may be a long-time acquaintance with whom you've spent much time, or it may be one of your own children. In your imagination realize that this person has never shown any interest in the Christian faith and couldn't care less about the kingdom of God. But, on this particular occasion, your friend comes to you and says: "*(Your name)*, you're a member of the church, right?" *(You affirm that.)* "And you are a Christian then and believe all that stuff?" *(Again, you answer yes.)* "O.K., tell me why. What's all this Jesus talk about and what difference does it make in your life?"

The exercise is to think through and write down for our own benefit a concise and convincing answer to that challenge. We do need to be ready to give an answer for our faith. We may never do it as well as we would like to, but we need to be ready. I am one of those people who always thinks after the fact of all the things I could have said if I had been sharper. But that doesn't mean that we can't begin to get our minds and hearts in gear for such an encounter.

People often think that because I am a pastor and a public person and a seminary-trained church leader I find witnessing to my faith something that comes easy. As a matter of fact I am a shy person, and I do not have the gift of evangelist. But I am a Christian. So people come to me as pastor, frequently total strangers, with all kinds of trouble and heartache, and pour them out on me in hopes that I will be some instant solution to their marital, economic, or vocational problems. I usually find it necessary to clear the air and let them know that I hear their pleas and that I do not have ready answers for everything. But I ask them if they will let me tell them who I am and why I am there. They almost always allow me this privilege. So I explain the grace of God, his love, and how I am there because of what God has done in Jesus Christ and not because the church hired me. I share my story and the grace of God and then ask if I can lift their problem to God in prayer. If there is any part I or the church can play in bringing real help, then I am obligated to do that. I am very thankful that, through my shy and fumbling efforts on such occasions as these, the Lord has brought salvation to people and also some amazingly redeemed characters and careers.

Prayer for Friends

Our enthusiasm over the gospel, our devotion to Christ, and our love for our non-Christian friends ought to constrain us to pray for them regularly. You ought to have a prayer list of at least three persons whom you know and with whom you have contact who have not yet come into God's family through faith in Jesus Christ. You ought to make a regular discipline of praying for alertness to other persons who may be desperately lost and looking for answers without even knowing it. There are a lot of people who appear to be happy pagans who are just shambles inside. They do not even know how to ask the right questions, so they sort of "fish around" in conversation, hoping that you will pick up the signals of their agony. We need to pray for perceptiveness to such needs.

All of this is to say that the work of calling persons out of darkness and into God's marvelous light belongs to each of us. Everyone of us has significant contact each week with probably two dozen people. By that I mean that in the course of our week we come into contact with the same persons in business or school or in the neighborhood, and so have access to them as persons. They should be at least in our prayers. We should be aware that we are on display before them and that they have the right to ask us for an answer.

Do you think this is just a Christian's fantasy of what non-Christians perceive about us? Then let me leave you with this quote from Albert Camus, who never was renowned as a professing Christian:

> The world expects of Christians that they will raise their voices so loudly and clearly and so formulate their protest that not even the simplest man can have the slightest doubt about what they are saying. Further, the world expects of Christians that they will eschew all fuzzy abstractions and plant themselves squarely in front of the bloody face of history. We stand in need of folk who have determined to speak directly and unmistakably and, come what may, to stand by what they have said.[6]

CHAPTER 15
The Mystery of Evangelism: Sowing, Watering, Reaping

Any way you look at the task of evangelization, it is fraught with the mystery of God's working. For centuries Christians have fallen all over themselves trying to figure out predestination, election, and such points of biblical teaching. Face it! The ways of God are inscrutable. The wonder and the mystery of his workings are written all over the course of human events. We rest in who he is. He is the faithful and the true. He is the God and Father of our Lord Jesus Christ. Therefore we do not live in dread that he will act capriciously or erratically or destructively. He has marvelously revealed his purpose to us in the coming of Jesus Christ. The mystery hid through the ages has been made known to us in God's Son. God has lavished his goodness upon us in Christ.

But that doesn't make God's workings any less mysterious to our finite minds. And not the least of this mystery is that God has chosen to use such instruments as we are in the work of evangelization. Here we are, clay pots all (2 Cor. 4:7). The apostle puts it a bit more euphemistically, but it is no less humbling: "But we have this treasure in earthen vessels, to show that the transcendent power belongs to God and not to us." Isn't it amazing that the task of heralding the news of the age to come, the kingdom of God, the grace and power of God in Jesus Christ, has been given to such ordinary folk as we are? The Lord rejoices to use the weak, the lowly born, the poor, and those of no reputation to be the instruments of the gospel. God: full of happy surprises!

Look at the roster of those in the Bible who were the agents of the tidings of great joy: a peasant girl named Mary, a group of rustics and an array of questionable others called disciples, eccentrics in the Old Testament called prophets, timid souls like Ananias who baptized Saul, cowards like Peter who became the Rock, aristocrats and diplomats like Isaiah and Daniel, quiet encouragers like Barnabas, a cook and waiter on tables named Philip who was an evangelist, and that host of nameless ones who prayed, talked to their neighbors, suffered, labored, took strangers into their homes, were imprisoned, loved, worshiped, and died that the message of the grace of God might be known by all people.

We focus on such commanding personalities as Saul of Tarsus who became Paul the Apostle—yet look at those who were used in his pilgrimage and in his ministry. There was the witness of the deacon Stephen, as he echoed the forgiving words of the dying Jesus at his own martyr's death while Saul stood by. There was the undoubted testimony of those dear, simple Christian folk whom Saul was harassing and imprisoning. There was Ananias, mentioned above, designated only as a disciple at Damascus, who against his own will became the first visitation evangelism practitioner as he sought an address where he was to speak the word of peace to Saul and to baptize him. There were those who sustained Paul through many years before he was sent forth on his first missionary journey, whose names we do not even know, and who yet were indispensable for his ministry.

I say all of this by way of encouragement. There is great mystery in the growth of God's kingdom. In his parables there are the numerous enigmatic statements that speak of the kingdom as being like the presence of leaven, or like a small seed growing into a large plant. It is a reality that comes not with observation but rather quietly. We tend to look for the spectacular and the dramatic which are much more observable. Yet the drama of the kingdom is that, against all kinds of opposition, in the most noncongenial settings, and by the instrumentality of the most unlikely persons, it grows and becomes a presence in demonstration of the will and power of God.

There is the mystery that the children of light dwell in the midst of the darkness and of the children of darkness. Though we share a common humanity with those of the darkness, we do not share a common perception with them. They see the immediate, the temporal—and are puzzled by it. We see eternal life, the kingdom of God. For us the light has come. We have a world and life view. We have hope. We know the God who is, who has become incarnate in Jesus Christ. They don't! They are always focusing on things, on experiences, on new schemes of self-help, on illusory panaceas, on threats, on demanding voices, and on themselves.

It is mystery! Jesus is the light come into a dark world. He by the working of the grace of God becomes our light and we are translated out of darkness and into his marvelous light. We then become the children of light "in the midst of a crooked and perverse generation among whom [we] shine as lights in the world" (Phil. 2:15). How does this happen? How are we the light of the world, we who are God's kingdom community?

Somehow as we live out our calling as the people of the joyous news many things happen. We become not only servants, and those who are truly human, and the light of the world, but we become disturbers. We expose the darkness and the works of darkness. This doesn't always make us the most popular of folks. We ask questions that probe and reveal. And we listen sensitively to our children, our friends, our neighbors, so that we can enter into significant conversation and discussion with them. We forthrightly speak of our persuasion of Jesus Christ and of the reality of his dominion and his salvation. Harking back to the prayer of St. Francis, we are those who love, who pardon, who believe, who hope, who enlighten, who rejoice, who console—we become the instruments of God's peace.

In all of this God is at work!

Living in the dominion of darkness are the Christian persons and the Christian communities who are the people of the kingdom of light and of God. God is at work in them and through them, making himself, his power, and his will known. He indwells them by his own life-giving Spirit, the Holy Spirit of God. As his people quietly and faithfully live under his word, then the light shines through their words and their holy lives so that they become his instruments of righteousness. And the Holy Spirit works through them to do that work of progressively shattering the darkness and pulling down the strongholds of Satan both in individual persons and in social structures of this age.

In contemplating the discipline of the work of evangelism, it is critical that we recognize the qualitative difference that distinguishes us from the children of darkness. We are not basically neutral persons with religious overtones. Not at all! We have entered new life under Christ's Lordship. He is at work in us by the Holy Spirit. Can you grasp the implication of this reality? The most modest underpaid employee, the widow on a pension, the worker on a coffee plantation, as well as the physician, the merchant, and the executive, have the same role in being children of light.

Each one sows, to use the figures from the parable of the sower and the seed. There is that initial work when the news of the kingdom of God is introduced to a person or a community for the first time. The response is not the issue. When the news is faithfully stated, no matter how falteringly or awkwardly, there is planted a seed that becomes somehow an opening for God to work in that community or person. That seed may lie apparently dormant for a long time. But God is at work.

How does one sow? It is just as we said above. We live out our calling as the new humanity of God in Christ. Our lives are lived in a relationship of integrity to him whom we love and adore. His character and his will become normative for our lives. We begin to respond to persons and situations as the children of our Father, in his likeness, or in holiness. It may be a deliberate introduction of a friend to the person of Jesus Christ. It may be an answer to a question, or the response to a crisis. But whenever we convey Jesus Christ in such a way that his person and work are communicated, the seed of the gospel is sown.

I am convinced that God's people are seldom conscious that

they are sowing the seed of the gospel. We tend to think of sowing as some very deliberate effort of sharing our witness with another, and this surely is sowing. But these are the exceptional moments of our lives. One of the first persons that I am aware of influencing for Christ (and I found this out months later) was a person who overheard a conversation that I was having with another Christian. I have found out in the years since that time that people have watched me, or listened at a distance, or shared in our family life, and have been implanted with a curiosity about the gospel. This is why our daily, wholesome, knowledgeable, joyous walk with the Lord is so crucial in what we're talking about.

And watering? Do the waterers know of the sowers? A personal hunch would be that they do not, ordinarily, though there is no reason why they may not. Yet in a life or a setting where the seed has been sown by a word or by some demonstration of the will of God, in that same setting at some subsequent time, the same or another Christian comes and confirms or corroborates the witness of the sower, and the seed is thereby watered. Again, you are dealing with mystery. You are dealing with that grace which comes before faith and conversion. You are dealing with that wind which blows where it wills (John 3:8).

Then reaping. The seed of the gospel germinates in a life, or a village, or a tribe, or a subculture, and there is faith where there was formerly unbelief. There is light where there was darkness. One of the Lord's people is there as a midwife, and helps the person or group of persons over the threshold of repentance and faith and into the kingdom of God. Or the sowing and watering may have raised questions and inspired a searching for answers, and at that appropriate moment something is said or done that brings light and gives the answer. Then Jesus is seen for who he is, God-made-flesh, and one is born anew into the family of God. In the mystery of that process the sower is as much a part as the waterer or the reaper; yet, ultimately, it is God who gives the increase and the praise belongs to him—God working in ordinary human beings such as we are, committing the treasure of the gospel to earthen vessels. Isn't that remarkable?

What is even more thrilling is that God doesn't just work through his kingdom people. God is the Lord of all and works by his own power and grace to produce hungerings, providentially to arrange incidents, to use cultural tides to make a people ready. God is not predictable or controllable, and this is what makes our calling to the work of evangelization such an adventure. In the most unlikely places and times we find that God has been there in ways we could not have imagined to prepare the soil for the sowing of the seed. No person, no situation, no culture can escape him. It is high adventure to be laboring together with God!

The dynamics of evangelism are mystery indeed. Yet the very mystery keeps us ever on tiptoe with expectation that our kingdom behavior and conversation will be the act of sowing or watering that will bring forth fruit to the praise of our glorious God.

Someone has said that the Christian life is a life of relaxed urgency. This is just to say that the urgency of our task is underscored by the costliness of our salvation: God spared not his own Son. We can be relaxed in the knowledge that as we faithfully walk with him, he works through us. Yet we can never become indifferent or lackadaisical toward the plight of those who are yet in darkness, who are the children of wrath. The fact that our lives may be modest and our efforts undramatic does not mean that the task is not urgent. The stewards of the gospel are required to be faithful, to be laboring, to be steadfast, to be abounding in the work of the Lord . . . until he comes. The apostle states it:

> So let us never tire of doing good, for if we do not slacken our efforts we shall in due time reap our harvest. Therefore, as opportunity offers, let us work for the good of all, especially members of the household of the faith.
>
> (Gal. 6:9–10, NEB)

CHAPTER 16
Making Contact

Let's speak directly to that outreach of the gospel of the kingdom that traditionally has been called either personal evangelism or one-on-one evangelism. Even though the Lord, our Redeemer and King, calls us into his kingdom *community* which is the church, yet he calls us one by one—he calls his sheep by name. All the propriety of giving prophetic kingdom witness to the structures and systems of darkness notwithstanding, still the Lord of all wants to confront *individuals* with himself through the gospel. Somehow in all of the history of the Christian church, the "bottom line" has been that moment when a child of the light has entered into a conversation with a child of darkness in order to bear the light to that person in the name of the Lord Jesus Christ.

My dream is not a congregation that contracts to be a part of some high-powered evangelistic program all wrapped in plastic. My dream is a congregation of down-to-earth, wholesome Christian folk who are "radioactive" with the love of Jesus Christ, who are alert to and praying for all of their non-Christian friends, and who are able to enter into gentle conversations with these friends which will bring them to the knowledge of the Lord in sensitive ways. I think this should be the norm.

Some researcher has determined (don't ask me how) that the average person has at least twelve significant contacts with other persons each week. That is to say that there are at least twelve persons with whom you and I dynamically interact each week. If this is true, it is possible that a significant percentage of these persons are not yet Christians. And this would mean that an ordinary congregation of one hundred-fifty members might have dynamic contact with several hundred not-yet-Christian persons each week. What a thrilling potential that holds for the work of evangelization and for the growth of the Christian community, the spread of the reign of God in lives.

Let's take it a step further. Earlier we mentioned a bit of church growth data which indicates that something over seventy percent of the persons who come to Christ and into the church come because a close friend or relative shares the knowledge of Christ with them and invites them into the church. That finding underscores the fact that our greatest potential field for evangelization is among persons who are very close to us, even related to us. There are natural bridges of friendship or family ties between us. It also indicates that these same persons are probably not going to be reached by the most able of professional evangelists, but rather by Christians like you and me.

We go to such elaborate schemes to bring the gospel of God's grace to those who don't know him, while all the time, they are our friends and relatives. I remember with some amusement an evangelistic Bible conference I participated in one summer. There was one thirteen-year-old boy who seemed impervious to the gospel. He was the terror of the conference. He surely knew that he was being conspired against by the whole Christian staff, hence some of his defensiveness and hostility. He probably felt like "a lion in a den of Daniels." One evening we had worked out a whole preaching meeting with him in view. We had prayed and worked out the components of the meeting with great detail and had the finest preacher in the conference on tap for the message.

It was only midway through the message that one perceptive person noticed that the boy was not even in the meeting. So while everyone else was basking in the meeting and in the fine preaching, this gentleman quietly slipped out and found the lonely boy, sat down next to him in the pine needles, and in warmth and love led him to Christ.

By the time the meeting was over all of the rest of the conference staff had recognized that the boy was not in the meeting and had begun to wring their hands and wonder what they had done wrong to allow Satan such a victory! After the meeting they were all standing around feeling defeated when the gentleman and the boy came in wreathed in smiles and shared the news of what God had done under a pine tree in the warmth of personal concern and quiet conversation.

Do you laugh or cry at such stories as this? Think of the multi-million dollar schemes, replete with the assistance of advertising agencies, that are regularly launched to evangelize the land. All the while the persons who need to know about what God has done in Christ have Christian friends whom they know and trust. In the United States there are reportedly eighty-nine million Christians and sixty million non-Christians (actually "churched" and "unchurched"). We know that at best these elaborate evangelistic programs reach a very small percentage of the people who need to hear. How then do we reach the "unchurched"? The answer is *us!*

Unless I am completely indifferent to non-Christian persons, the joyous task is mine. If I am indifferent then I am guilty of a gospel disobedience that is spiritually perilous. The Holy Spirit in you and me is the Spirit of Jesus who came to seek and to save the lost. Get the message?

So here we are with these close friends and relatives who are not yet Christians. Who are they? Where do we meet them? Where and how do the children of light interact with the children of darkness?

At this point I am assuming that you are a deliberate Christian, a person who is unashamedly the Lord's and a citizen of the kingdom of God. I am assuming that the teachings covered in section two of this book on spiritual formation are your experience. All right! Let's begin to look at some basic steps for sharing the good news with those others whom we desire to know the glad tidings of great joy.

A Strategy of Prayer

An Indian Christian brother laid down the principle some years back that prayer is the beginning of evangelism. "If you have not prayed for your non-Christian friends, you have not even begun the work of evangelization." In your own personal prayer times this needs to be a regular item:

1. Lord, who are my non-Christian acquaintances? Who do I meet regularly who needs to know of your love? Who in my circle of friends? in my family?

2. Lord, where do I find myself each week? in what places? with what social, professional, occupational, or community groups? Where do I have dynamic contact and input?

3. Lord, what kind of impact and influence do I have among those who know me? Are my behavior and conversation such as become a member of your family and a citizen in your kingdom? Am I indifferent to your will for the persons I meet? Am I careless about your desire to see my friends come into your great salvation? Are there places you want to refine me?

Make a list of the persons that come to mind and make them a matter of prayer. If you do no more than ask the Father in heaven that they may come to know him, that is a good beginning. But beyond that, there is a promise that if we seek, and knock, and ask, the Father will be faithful to give the Holy Spirit in answer. I interpret that passage in Luke 11 to have importance for the work of evangelism. Look at the way this comes out:

> Then [Jesus] said to them, "Suppose one of you has a friend who comes to him in the middle of the night and says, 'My friend, lend me three loaves, for a friend of mine on a journey has turned up at my house, and I have nothing to offer him'; and he replies from inside, 'Do not bother me. The door is shut for the night; my children and I have gone to bed; and I cannot get up and give you what you want.' I tell you that even if he will not provide for him out of friendship, the very shamelessness of the

request will make him get up and give him all he needs. And so I say to you, ask, and you will receive; seek, and you will find; knock, and the door will be opened. For everyone who asks receives, he who seeks finds, and to him who knocks, the door will be opened.

"Is there a father among you who will offer his son a snake when he asks for fish, or a scorpion when he asks for an egg? If you, then, bad as you are, know how to give your children what is good for them, how much more will the heavenly Father give the Holy Spirit to those who ask him!"

(Luke 11:5–13, NEB)

I know there have been several ways of interpreting this passage. But I have to accept the one that understands it as a promise to us in situations where, in our ministry to others, we do not humanly have the resources to meet their needs. For those resources we are to ask. In our ministry of evangelism we recognize that the need is for a work of grace and enlightening and convicting in the non-Christian person. That has to be a work of the Spirit of God, and we are encouraged here to go to our Father who can grant that petition to his children. In our labors, we are obeying the Lord with all of our human limitations, but we are also aware of the sovereign and mysterious working of the Spirit in the human heart and mind. Therefore, as we have our prayer list of friends, we make supplication to our Father that he will be working in those friends by the Spirit to make them ready to hear and to receive the word of the gospel.

The other side of the coin is that we also pray that we will, by the enabling of the Holy Spirit, be made very sensitive to those other persons. We need to be aware of what is going on in them, of where their hearts and minds are, of where their resistance to truth may be, of how they may have been scarred somewhere along the line, of what their gods or gospels may be. Our prayer here, then, is for ourselves. We do not want to be crude, unlistening, monological, insensitive assaulters of persons with the gospel. Rather, we want to be gentle, bold, and compassionate bearers of the joyous news of God's love and kingdom to our friends. To get a vivid illustration of what this prayer means, all one needs to do is look at those dozen or so episodes where Jesus encountered individuals. He could be very firm, almost abrupt, where the occasion called for it; or he could be wonderfully gentle and caring. But all of his responses came out of his redemptive love. So we must pray that the Holy Spirit will pour out the love of God into our hearts and through our human lives to others.

An Understanding of Witness

What is a "witness" for Christ? Is he a person with a memorized methodology of witnessing to someone else, replete with Bible verses? Is she a person with a canned testimony that she drops on everybody she can? Is it an outgoing person with the persuasive ability of a salesperson and a ready tongue? Well, face it! It may be. God uses many diverse instruments to do his work.

But let me make a confession. I'm on the side of the anti-heroes. I believe that most of us who love Jesus and who desire to be faithful in our witness to him and to his kingdom are, to state it flatly, just well-intentioned klutzes. I don't mean anything pejorative by that. We are just happy Christians who commit our awkwardness to the Lord and by his grace make the best of our limitations. Most of us don't have a lot of style. We don't have eloquent tongues and well-chosen phrases. The only thing unique about us is the grace of God in our lives, which has called us out of darkness and into his marvelous light. We are, and intend to be, genuine human beings, who share humanity with our friends. But we are human beings who have made a life-changing discovery. That discovery is Jesus Christ. He has transformed our understanding of who we are and what's going on here, and our whole outlook on life and the world!

We don't even understand all we know about Jesus Christ. We know that before we ever discovered him, he found us. We have conflicts within ourselves between some lingering rebellion against God that keeps bubbling up from the recesses of our

lives and the desire to love and obey God that is the evidence
of his new creation in us. We certainly are not boasting perfection in our Christian lives. We continue to be sinners and saved
at the same time. We are children of grace, dependent daily
upon the forgiveness and mercy of God. Yet we are alive and
enlightened and free, because we have truly entered into God's
new order and have been sealed with the Holy Spirit, who is the
guarantee of our redemption.

So how do we witness to others? Witness is not some religious "snow job" through which we try, humanly, to manipulate another person into the kingdom of God. It is not that at
all. The apostle states it this way:

> We use no hocus-pocus, no clever tricks, no dishonest
> manipulation of the Word of God. We speak the plain
> truth and so commend ourselves to every man's con-
> science in the sight of God.
>
> (2 Cor. 4:2, J. B. Phillips)

That sort of sums it up. A witness is one who can relate with
faithfulness and accuracy what God has said and done. As a
witness to others about Jesus Christ, I am just conveying to
them my own understanding and wonder at what God has
provided in Jesus Christ, and at what God has done in my own
experience. I am making a statement of fact. The inauguration
of the kingdom of God and the accomplishment of redemption
in Jesus Christ is not an opinion; it is a fact. My persuasion of that
fact and my own experience of repentance and faith are also
facts. That Jesus has transformed my life and thinking and values is more than a subjective opinion; it is a matter of record.
Because of this, I am willing to talk about Jesus to my friends.
I am also willing to be questioned and cross-examined about my
knowledge of and experience of him.

Within the context of friendship, there is nothing amiss
about sharing my experience with Jesus Christ. After all, it is the
most significant thing about my life. That I am a child of God
is not a fact that I can easily hide, nor do I want to. So I might
easily say something like this to a friend:

"Marylou, we have been riding in this car-pool for eight months now, and our conversations have always gone in dozens of directions, from leaking faucets to foreign policy. The real news that excites me is the news of how God has made himself known in Jesus. Would you be interested in how I became aware of this?"

I have a feeling that most people are very much interested, but I believe we need to give friends the option as to whether they want to hear or not. At the very least, we are making ourselves available to discuss it with them. If our Marylou were to say, "Yes, I am interested," then we could proceed to tell our story of faith. If, on the other hand, she says, "I'm not interested in that religious talk," then, we can counter by saying that we understand, but that if she ever wants to sit down and discuss the subject of Jesus Christ we are available.

We need to let our friends know of our interest in them, and of our enthusiasm about God and the gospel. We should not be flapped by the non-Christians' irreverence, or by their often blasphemous comments. We need to be ready, with all modesty, to at least hear, and if possible to discuss, their objections or their misgivings. We need to realize that behind what appear to be unfriendly statements is very often a spiritual hungering that is cautiously seeking an answer that is faithful. The answer they're looking for is Jesus Christ; but if they've got some misconception of him, or if they've been the victims of some religious manipulation in times past, then they are understandably cautious, even defensive.

More often, our friends are really curious about Jesus Christ, and, given the right setting, would like to talk about him with us. I suppose I get more responses to a low-key invitation like this than to any other:

"Hey, I want you to know that I'm really excited about Jesus Christ, and if you'd like to, I'd love to sit down with you sometime and share my excitement with you."

We're not posing as "know-it-alls" either. Just real human beings who have come into contact with Jesus Christ and through him have come into God's new order, into salvation, into a whole new quality of life. We're not necessarily experts (though we ought to be working in that direction), but we are honest witnesses of what we have seen, heard, and experienced of the Word of life. We need to work this out in such a way that we are true to ourselves and to the Lord, so that our witness is our own and has the ring of integrity and authenticity. I may be a well-intentioned klutz with all the awkwardness that implies, but I do very much want to be genuine and authentically Christian.

The Setting for Witness

There really aren't any rules as to where you will find the best setting for your Christian witness. But there are some observations and some principles that will make you alert to possibilities. Some people are public persons and often have forums such as civic groups or clubs or professional gatherings. Such forums, used wisely, present a rare opportunity. I believe that such opportunities are the exception rather than the norm, but I am thankful for them. I was on an airline with a friend recently who was bemoaning the fact that he couldn't find his slot in a local congregation. As the conversation shifted it came out that he was a motivational speaker for one of the largest corporations in the world. He traveled all over the world making addresses, in which it was quite natural for him to use his own Christian faith as an illustration. As he shared with me this "illustration" I realized that God had given him a place of public witness that had staggering implications. This was his ministry on behalf of the church. The local congregation, rather than making him feel guilty, ought to turn him loose to this ministry and pray for him in it. He is an international ambassador for God.

Most of us operate in much more modest circles of contact. We find our friends close to home. I believe that the witness of the Christian to a non-Christian friend involves real spiritual conflict, as light confronts darkness, and for this reason I think we should at least seek the most hospitable and convivial setting

available to do this. It is almost amusing to look at the settings
for so much of the Christian conversation and witness of the
New Testament folk: the edge of a well, a wedding party, the
dinner table, a picnic for five thousand, and house to house
visitation.

For this reason I like to avoid sterile settings, opting for a
conversation over a meal or a cup of coffee. That is very biblical.
It is a tradition that is as old as the Christian church. Is there
anything unspiritual about providing the niceties of human
kindness as we share the news of Jesus Christ with those for
whom we care? People feel more relaxed when food and drink
are present because these are physical expressions of our caring.
I have seen very perceptive articles on this subject entitled
"Knife and Fork Evangelism" or "Spaghetti Evangelism." The
point is that whenever the choice is yours to make, choose a
friendly place to talk to your friends about Christ.

This brings us to an observation from church history. The
major place in which evangelism was done in the early church
and has been done over the centuries since is the Christian
home. Your home, be it a modest cottage, an apartment, or a
manor house, ought to be the setting for you to provide hospitality, refuge, thoughtful conversation, and the gospel to your
friends. An open home is a principle that comes through in the
Bible from beginning to end. "Be given to hospitality"—show
it to saints and to strangers—is a New Testament principle. Why
is this so important? For starts, it shows our concern for the
physical and emotional needs of another. Every Christian family is a small demonstration of God's family, and of the caring
of our Father-Mother God (Ps. 27:10). Our Christian homes,
with their warmth, kitchens, dinner tables, extra beds, and love
ought to be looked upon not as showplaces but as manifestations
of the caring of God.

The people who come under your roof may be poor and
needy physically, financially, emotionally, or spiritually, or all of
these. Frequently what a person needs is not a speech or a
lecture but a place of refuge and of love. When a person sits
down at your table or sleeps in your spare bed and enjoys the

sanctuary of your loving home, then defenses begin coming
down. There is a receptivity to hearing what it is that makes
your home like it is, and that something is God's love in Jesus
Christ

There are many things that make the Christian home such
a unique setting for the work of evangelism:

1. *The atmosphere of faith,* which comes through in
family worship, prayers at meals, and family celebrations, as well as in the conversations.

2. *The family atmosphere of love,* which must be genuine and honest. The members of the family must genuinely care for each other and for those in the home.
Handling of differences, resolving of conflicts, the servant spirit, as well as the humor and hilarity, all reflect
this loving atmosphere.

3. *The decorations and literature of the home.* Archa-
eologists have been interested in finding that Christian
homes from very early periods are discernable because
of Christian symbols and inscriptions, which are still
there in frescoes and mosaics. While these were undoubtedly indications to other Christians as to the faith of those
in the home, they must have also aroused the curiosity
and inquiry of outsiders. So the flavor of a home is clearly
indicated by what hangs on the walls and by what sits on
the bookshelf. Conversation starters among the decorations of our homes are most useful. Our homes should
reflect our kingdom citizenship and values.

I have spent this much time on the Christian home as the
setting of evangelistic witness just because it is such an available
setting to most of us. We meet people in a nonthreatening way
in our homes. Our neighbors drop in to borrow something, or
to have a cup of tea. Our friends come over for a meal or for
games. Our children bring their friends home from school. An
acquaintance comes by to share a crisis. Somebody needs a
place to stay for a few nights. Lord, make our homes places of
kingdom hospitality and Christian witness!

I am of the opinion that in this country during the past two decades home Bible study has become one of the most un-heralded means of bringing the gospel to non-Christian people. Christians will invite their friends in for coffee and to read and discuss the Bible almost as a social occasion. People who would never darken the door of a church building will respond to the low-key friendly atmosphere of a gathering in a home. There is also a general curiosity about the content of the Bible. So people have come in huge numbers to these countless home Bible studies. I know of very few of these Bible studies where some-one has not found Christ and come crashing into the kingdom of God with rejoicing.

Wherever you meet your non-Christian friends, though, becomes the locus for your Christian witness. I have heard of people joyfully witnessing in pubs, on sailboats, in country clubs, over a lunch pail, in a sauna bath, over the back fence, and in scores of other unusual places. Use to the glory of God those places where you meet people!

Midwifery

Kingdom witnesses also need to be equipped to be the mid-wives who assist their friends as they are "birthed" into the kingdom of God. If and when, as a result of a Christian witness, a friend asks—"How do I come into God's kingdom? How do I become a Christian? How do I experience the forgiveness and love of God?"—then we need to be prepared to walk with the person through the disciplines of repentance, faith, and bap-tism, and to stand by that friend as he or she grows in Christian discipleship. We have gone over this already *(see chapter nine),* but it deserves a reminder here.

You will recognize that there are many avenues of evange-lism and of Christian missions that I might have explored in this chapter. I have chosen the avenue of personal contact because of a proclivity which many writers on the subject have to emphasize the dramatic, the ideal, and the unusual. I am persuaded that the task of communicating the gospel of the kingdom is done primarily by ordinary Christians, with ordinary equipment, under ordinary circumstances. This is one of the marvels of God's plan for the ages.

> "To what shall I compare the kingdom of God? It is like leaven which a woman took and hid in three measures of flour, till it was all leavened."
>
> (Luke 13:20–21)

It is not the dramatic and the grandiose of large programs of evangelization that get the work done. It is the mysterious chemistry of countless ordinary Christians faithfully living out their kingdom lives. These share their faith in Jesus Christ and interact with their friends. By the working of the Spirit the darkest recesses and the uttermost corners of the world are touched by the gospel of the kingdom. Hallelujah!

CHAPTER 17
The Systems of Evil and the Hapless Victims

At the beginning of this volume we enumerated as the problem several of the faces of sin. We spoke of personal evil, interpersonal evil, systemic evil, and then of the hapless victims of systemic evil. These dimensions of the dominion of darkness are unmistakable in the biblical teachings. Yet when we speak of evangelism we dwell almost solely on the first two, on the redemption of persons and the creation of a new community, which is the church. There's nothing amiss about that. That is exactly where the Bible puts the emphasis. It still leaves us, however, with a question as to whether there is some redemptive involvement we are to have with the systems of evil and the hapless victims of the systems of evil.

Because the gospel of the kingdom of God has cosmic implications, we cannot dwell only on individuals. Since the new age of God has invaded the present we cannot rest content where his will and name are profaned in evil systems. Nor can we shut out the cries of the victims and still come before God in prayer. With all of this around us, what are we to do? It is not enough just to feel guilty, or to be cynical. Does the joyous news of the kingdom of God have any bearing on such systems and their victims?

Let me hold up a scripture passage to give us some context for this discussion:

> For I reckon that the sufferings we now endure bear no comparison with the splendour, as yet unrevealed, which is in store for us. For the created universe waits with

191

eager expectation for God's sons to be revealed. It was made the victim of frustration, not by its own choice, but because of him who made it so; yet always there was hope, because the universe itself is to be freed from the shackles of mortality and enter upon the liberty and splendour of the children of God. Up to the present, we know, the whole created universe groans in all its parts as if in the pangs of childbirth. Not only so, but even we, to whom the Spirit is given as firstfruits of the harvest to come, are groaning inwardly while we wait for God to make us his sons and set our whole body free. For we have been saved, though only in hope. Now to see is no longer to hope: why should a man endure and wait for what he already sees? But if we hope for something we do not yet see, then, in waiting for it, we show our endurance.

(Rom. 8:18–25, NEB)

". . . The created universe waits . . . the victim of frustration . . . the whole created universe groans in all its parts. . . ." Such statements express our agony as those who live between the ages. The inauguration of the kingdom of God has given us hope. We have tasted of the good things of the age to come by the Holy Spirit. Yet the kingdom has not yet been consummated. We live in the presence of the tragic, of the defilement of this present age. We know that at the end the kingdoms of this world will become the kingdoms of our God and of his Christ. But it is not yet. And so we endure. But are we to be passive? While we groan and are frustrated with the rest of creation, how do we express our zeal for the glory of God in his creation?

There is no question that the example set for us by Jesus and the apostles puts some kind of priority on that witness to the gospel that brings individuals into the community of faith. But then Paul makes the statement, which we looked at earlier, that through the church the manifold wisdom of God is made known to principalities and powers. His statement is one of the New Testament clues to the fact that the church is somehow to impact the power structures that are related to the dominion of darkness. This is also part of our witness. But how do we do it?

There is no easy answer to this very demanding question. There is no nice, clean New Testament example or teaching along this line. We endure. We see the saints under the altar in the book of Revelation crying out, "How long, O Lord?" and we share that cry with them. I want only to address a few remarks, not to individuals but to the Christian community, about our sojourn in the midst of this present age.

We are those who, as we gather week by week, pray to our Father in heaven: "Thy kingdom come, Thy will be done on earth as it is in heaven." This very prayer is integrally related to the whole discipline of evangelism. It is the prayer of God's kingdom people, who are aware of the joyous news of who God is, of what he has done in Jesus Christ, and of his ultimate purpose to make all things new. It is the prayer of the Christian community which is aware of the dynamic presence of the kingdom of God here and now. A quote by the late Professor Norval Geldenhuys will be useful at this point:

> "Thy kingdom come." This might be better rendered: "Let thy divine rule come." The prayer is that the Father's divine sovereignty should more and more fully attain its rightful place in the heart and life of fallen mankind, who otherwise are bound under the sway of the powers of darkness; that instead of living in sin and rebellion against God men should be brought to live their whole life more and more under the control of God's sovereign rule. So this supplication refers to the extension of the divine dominion in the life of mankind in this age. But in the highest instance it is a supplication that the kingly dominion of God which came with power into the life of mankind in the first coming of Jesus shall come in full glory and perfection through Christ's second coming. "Thy will be done, as in heaven, so on earth." This supplication . . . is practically a closer description of the preceding supplication. In heaven God's will is obeyed by all, spontaneously, with the deepest joy and in a perfect manner without a shadow of unfaithfulness. And the believer must pray that such a condition should also prevail on earth. Already in this age this supplication is being heard, but only when the "new earth" appears and the powers of

evil have been destroyed, the will of God will be obeyed by all in fullness and perfection.[7]

This is the prayer of the Christian community. It is a prayer of struggle in the battle between the dominion of darkness and the dominion of light. It is an evangelizing prayer. It is a prayer of hope. It is a prayer that has telling ethical implications since we are the people of God's kingdom and the agents of his will.

The Lord's Prayer also does not assume that darkness and light are always easily distinguishable. We all know how easily we are conformed to this age, how easily the light in us becomes darkness. So the Lord teaches us to pray: "Lead us not into temptation, but deliver us from (the) evil." We in the Christian community, as the people of the gospel, need to pray for the grace to keep our vision clear, to distinguish between darkness and light in our daily pilgrim walk through this darkness.

The Christian community begins the work of demonstrating the gospel to principalities, to the systems of evil, in its life of prayer. It is while the community is gathered for prayer that it holds up to God its petitions for his kingdom and his will to be manifested here and now. It is in prayer that the community lifts up the hapless victims of the systems of injustice and unrighteousness to the Father. Together the community struggles to know what gospel obedience is in each locale and in each new day. It is in prayer that the community's faith is translated into works. It is in the prayer life of the community that the love of God takes on form so that the real needs of real persons shall be met.

One wise Christian brother said that every Christian ought to have devotions with the Bible in one hand and the daily newspaper in the other. Behind this is the concern that Christians be alert both to the word of God and to the real world in which we live as the people of God. I pass this along to the Christian community as we come to grips with that area of evangelism where the kingdom of God confronts the systems of evil and seeks to be faithful in caring for the hapless victims of these systems of evil.

Any discerning reader can tell that I am walking very cautiously through this area. It has never been easy or safe for the church to be faithful here. It is here that the Dragon does warfare against the Lamb. It is here that the community of the Great King becomes a disturbing force. It is here, also, that costly discipleship often brings tensions and makes demands that—alas!—divide even the community of faith. It is no big thing to make lofty ecclesiastical deliverances against the wrongs of society. The people of darkness can live with our altruistic verbiage and our easy pronouncements. It is when Christian people get into the arena of real life and flesh out their kingdom concerns with action that the warfare waxes hot.

But we dare not be silent! The mandates of the kingdom of God are upon us now. If there is any area where we need to come at a challenge as a community it is this one. An individual Christian may by the grace of God bear a significant witness to the structures of darkness; but this is an area of evangelism where we need the support, prayers, and corporate expression of the community of faith. The global problems of economic injustice, of unrighteousness in politics, of the vast wasteland of criminology and penology, of cultural darkness, of advancing secularism in public education, of a pathological materialism and consumerism, and of the plight of the unimaginable number of the world's poor are so staggering that we are liable to be paralyzed into inaction.

Yet . . .

> This is my Father's world:
> Oh, let me ne'er forget
> That though the wrong seems oft so strong,
> God is the Ruler yet.[8]

So there are three perspectives that I wish to lay before the Christian community. These are disciplines that will assist us in responding to the joyous news of the kingdom, thus being instruments of evangelization in the midst of the dominion of darkness and the systemic evil of this age

The Perspective of the Word of God

It is important to keep in focus what God has on his mind with reference to this world in which we live. When we use the word *evangelism,* we are prone to use it lightly, assuming that it means creating a more comfortable spiritual climate for ourselves by creating a larger Christian majority in our community. There is certainly nothing wrong with wanting to see more of our acquaintances come into the household of faith, even if our motives might be a bit selfish in doing so.

But God obviously has something else on his heart, which comes through in scripture with such clout that we dare not ignore it. I speak of the references to the implementation of justice and righteousness and to the concern for the poor of this world. God's compassionate care for the poor and helpless of this world is a major teaching of scripture that is almost entirely overlooked by all too many of us in the Christian community. There are over four hundred passages numbering over a thousand verses in the Bible that deal with God's concern for the poor. Issues of justice for the oppressed are tied right into this concern, along with God's intention to see righteous dealings within the human community. God's displeasure is expressed over and over against those who ignore such.

Throughout the Old Testament there is the concern that the stranger be given refuge in the homes of God's people, and that provision be made for those who are poor. There is the gleaning law, and the law of just weights. Because many poor would sell themselves into slavery, there was the provision of the jubilee year when all the slaves went free so that no one would be in perpetual slavery.

The Israelites forgot this all too soon. You have an eighth-century prophet like Isaiah speaking the word of the Lord to his people, and his message deals with their inhumane response to those in need. Oh, they had religion aplenty, but it was all external and missed the point of God's concern for his people: "Behold, in the day of your fast you seek your own pleasure, and oppress all your workers" (Isa. 58:3). Then he proceeds with this

prophetic word that harks back to the covenant by which God
had called them to be his people:

> "Is not this the fast that I choose:
>   to loose the bonds of wickedness,
>   to undo the thongs of the yoke,
> to let the oppressed go free,
>   and to break every yoke?
> Is it not to share your bread with the hungry,
>   and to bring the homeless poor into your house;
> when you see the naked, to cover him,
>   and not to hide yourself from your own flesh?
> Then shall your light break forth like the dawn,
>   and your healing shall spring up speedily;
> your righteousness shall go before you,
>   the glory of the LORD shall be your rear guard.
> Then you shall call, and the LORD will answer;
>   you shall cry, and he will say, Here I am."
>
> (Isa. 58: 6–9)

Is it not altogether possible and probable that the objects of
our evangelistic concern and our kingdom ministry should be
primarily those who are among the helpless and poor? It is not
that the comfortable and rich are not in need of God's redeeming grace also, or that they should be neglected, but rather that
a priority should be placed upon those who have a special place
in God's heart. Established middle-class churches that wonder
why they are not under God's blessing in their life and growth
might do well to ponder this passage from Isaiah.

In the same section of Isaiah we have before us the passage
which Jesus later quoted of himself in the synagogue at
Nazareth. Here is the purpose of his anointing:

> The Spirit of the Lord GOD is upon me,
>   because the LORD has anointed me
> to bring good tidings to the afflicted;
>   he has sent me to bind up the brokenhearted,
> to proclaim liberty to the captives,
>   and the opening of the prison to those who are bound;
> to proclaim the year of the LORD's favor,
>   and the day of vengeance of our God;
> to comfort all who mourn. . . ."   (Isa. 61:1–2)

It should not escape us that the objects of Jesus' anointed ministry of evangelization are the victims of the systems of evil. That such systems exist is undoubtedly accepted as a fact by Jesus and the prophets. It is the victims of such that are of particular concern to God. When Jesus quoted this passage in Nazareth (Luke 4) he followed the reading by saying: "Today this scripture has been fulfilled in your hearing."

Our kingdom calling gives us a very clear word from our King as to his zeal that "justice roll down like waters, and righteousness like an ever-flowing stream" (Amos 5:24). We know of his zeal for the poor and the helpless. God's kingdom people will use every means at their disposal to see the kingdom mandates accomplished. We will be co-belligerents with all others, Christians or non-Christians, who seek the same ends. Yet, in a unique way, the Christian community will identify with these victims and flesh out the principles of the kingdom, thus demonstrating right in the face of principalities and powers what is the nature of God's plan.

We are not so much social activists as *kingdom* activists. We are here to demonstrate good news, to evangelize in a costly way, those who are the victims of the dominion of darkness. And if this seems to be a bit radical, then one should look at such passages as Matthew 11:1–6, where Jesus rehearses the signs of the kingdom to the disciples of John, including that one concerning the poor having the gospel preached to them.

Even more telling is Matthew 25:31–46, where Jesus speaks of his return and judgment of the nations. The basis of his judgment includes nothing at all of what we ordinarily consider evangelistic credentials, but rather has to do with our faithfulness in being his ministers to the poor, the naked, the hungry, the sick, and the imprisoned. What do you make of that?

The perspective of the Word of God demands of us that we keep clearly in focus where biblical priorities are; and it shakes our middle-class assumptions to the foundations. Our Christian press revels in those rich and famous persons who make Christian professions. Our mainline denominations rush in competition to locate new churches in the prosperous neighborhoods. All too often we trample the epistle of James underfoot as we fall all over ourselves to attract and please the rich. And what happens when we do this is that we become part of the darkness. When the church identifies with the rich it axiomatically is locked into the oppressive darkness. All the while, Jesus is pointing us elsewhere.

Add to this the historical fact that cultures have seldom, if ever, been evangelized and transformed from the top, the upper class, down. Rather, they have been evangelized and transformed from the lower classes up.

We must insist upon the perspective of the Word of God as we live as the community of faith in the presence of the darkness. This particular focus on the poor seems so neglected that it is worthy of special note. It is not that God is unconcerned about the middle class, the comfortable, and the secure. He comes to seek and to save the lost, whoever they may be. But God makes demands of repentance upon the comfortable that are costly, because they are so often, though perhaps unknowingly, agents in the systems of economic and political injustice. The demands of the kingdom are radical indeed.

The Perspective of What's Going On in the World

A local Christian community can easily become an anachronism, or even worse, a cultural "ghetto," by being oblivious to history and to the God of history. Citizens in God's kingdom, by the very nature of their calling, need to be alert to what is going on in the world around them, in the dominion of darkness and of Satan. If we do not keep aware of the setting of our kingdom calling, then we become, as one wit put it: "so heavenly-minded that we are of no earthly use"!

The Chronicler speaks of the men of Issachar "who had understanding of the times, to know what Israel ought to do . . ." (1 Chron. 12:32). The Christian community desperately needs persons of that vision so that we will be on the cutting edge of society and not merely reactionaries. Kingdom evangelists need to have eyes to perceive the future as well as the present. Surely we should not be dwelling in the past. Unfortunately, it is much easier in hindsight to see what we might have done than to pray for some foresight and some prophetic sense as to how to meet the challenges of today and tomorrow.

For instance, we look back with pain at the thirteenth century when the great Kublai Khan, ruler of the Mongols, sent a request to the pope for one hundred men skilled in the Christian religion, so that he and his great men and people might become Christians. Only two ever started and they turned back, so the Mongol hordes became, for the most part, Muslims. In hindsight we see that Asia might have been a predominantly Christian continent, except that no one had the vision to see it then.

In the 1960's, the youth of the United States were in ferment. All that most people in the church could see were "dirty hippies" who had no respect for the institutions, traditions, and promises of the land. Yet these youth were bitter over the Vietnam war and eagerly seeking some more meaningful life in the "Age of Aquarius." Very few Christians had the understanding to sense that there was a great spiritual hunger being expressed. And so the "Jesus Revolution," one of the great revivals of church history, took place, for the most part, outside of the established church. In the aftermath, one Christian wrote a book entitled *Where Was the Church When the Youth Exploded?*[9] Again we look back and wonder how we missed the signals.

In discerning the times, as people with the news of joy to the world, we've got to remember that the joyous news is of God and that he is not idling around in the world passively waiting for us to get our act together. I am inclined to believe that our God has a riotous sense of humor just in the way he shows his saving purpose. He converted the great persecutor of the church, Paul, and it was so contrary to what the church thought could ever happen that it took them years to believe it was for real. And dear old kosher Peter, all hung up with the old covenant, was used to break the barrier and to see Gentile Cornelius

and his "unclean" Gentile household all converted and evi-
dencing their new life in the Spirit in unmistakable ways. So it
has been down through church history.

There is a principle in scripture that indicates that wherever
the defilement of sin increases, there God causes his grace also
to abound, so that grace "might reign through righteousness to
eternal life through Jesus Christ our Lord" (Rom. 5:20–21). This
means that God rejoices to work where the darkness is the
greatest. The Christian community, then, needs to look for
those areas where the darkness is increasing upon us, or where
the darkness is the darkest, and take the gospel there. Too often
we have tended to shy away from assaults upon the bastions of
darkness, and have maintained polite spirituality and tepid
evangelism in the more secure environs of proper folk like
ourselves.

Yet, if the light has shined into the darkness in Jesus Christ,
and if we, by our calling, are the light of the world in him, then
we ought to be seeking out those areas of cultural darkness, and
aggressively finding ways to herald the grace of God and the
power of God through the gospel.

The catalog of such areas is not difficult to come by for
anyone who prayerfully keeps a finger on the pulse of the news.
Here are a few:

> *Families in crisis.* In every strata of society there is a
> deterioration of family life with all the long-range psy-
> chological and sociological consequences of this break-
> down.
>
> *Marriage in crisis.* The escalating divorce rate, the near
> legalization of living together arrangements outside of
> marriage, the undermining effect of narcissism on mar-
> riage, and other cultural pressures make marriage a criti-
> cal area in our society.
>
> *Women in search of identity.* Apart from all the legal
> issues of E.R.A. and the pro and con discussions over
> feminism and women's rights, there is an obvious search
> going on by great numbers of women as to their own
> significance, and a deep hungering for fulfillment.

The proliferation of religious cults. When you look into the teachings and offerings of most cults, you realize that a person has to be desperately in search of almost any straw of meaning, or clue to fulfillment, to get involved in them. Yet the response to these religions of darkness is frightening.

Narcissism. All the psychological self-help books and the packaged therapy techniques evidence a preoccupation with self that is looking in the wrong place for the answer and is tragically deceptive.

Homosexuality. Hundreds of thousands of persons in recent years have "come out of the closet" and acknowledged openly that they are homosexual, trying to defend that as a valid lifestyle. For all the protests, the hard data indicates that homosexuality is psychologically and emotionally destructive. Yet these are real and usually very sensitive persons crying out for acceptance.

We could go on to mention the aging, the single young adults, the ethnic minorities, the helpless poor, the homeless children, and others. Every community has within it those areas where the moral, ethical, and spiritual darkness is obvious. Lest we be like the Pharisees, who stand aside and pull their garments around them for fear of being defiled, we will begin praying our way into the work of bringing light into this darkness.

And in every community there is that systemic darkness that needs to be discerned, and to which the Christian community must address itself as the community of the kingdom of God. There is political darkness, economic injustice and oppression, jurisprudential darkness, ecological disaster. We have the enormous problems of our cities, which look almost hopeless from some perspectives. Whatever violates, or profanes, God's creation is by its very nature the concern of the community of God's own. Wherever real human beings are being systematically dehumanized, oppressed, or destroyed, the good news of God's new order must address itself.

There is no simple formula for the discipline of knowing what is going on in the world, but a discipline of urgency it surely is. The Christian community concerned with kingdom evangelism dare not neglect it.

The Perspective of a Versatile and Flexible Church

In the work of evangelism, there is little purpose in having the perspective of the Word of God, or the perspective of what's going on in the world, if the Christian community is so rigid and unresponsive that it is not able to flex to meet the challenge or to innovate for a new opportunity. We are never guaranteed that efforts will be successful, even if we are flexible and versatile. We know that the gospel of God brings us into confrontation with the darkness. But every new age and every different culture and subculture makes its own demands on the church as to how that unchangeable gospel is presented. The church is part of the new wine of the gospel, of which Jesus spoke. The form of the church, to use Jesus' figure, is not of the essence of the new wine but is only a wineskin. It is that form, that wineskin, that we must be continually evaluating as to its usefulness in being a viable vehicle for the message in a given situation.

There is nothing especially spiritual about Elizabethan English, Gothic architecture, eighteenth-century hymns, the organizational models of corporate America, or a Master of Divinity degree from a theological school. None of these are guarantees of anything. They may be very useful in one place and a disaster in another. They are part of the traditions and heritage of the Christian community in our Western culture. In another culture they are not even recognized.

Case in point. I happen to be a Presbyterian. Our Presbyterian denomination is self-consciously middle class. We can afford comfortable church buildings. We require an educated pastoral ministry. We organize our congregations like we organize our businesses or our civic groups. We are at ease with budgetary matters, goal setting, and responsible finance. But if we identify these with kingdom priorities, we do ourselves a disservice. These may all be very useful to our middle-class culture, but they are not part of the gospel.

The mistake we make is in trying to superimpose these accouterments upon those who are not of our middle-class ethos. The area of the country in which I live is between thirty and forty percent poor. This means that something in excess of a third of the population comes under the category of "poverty level." If we Presbyterians are unwilling to be flexible, then we try to take the gospel to these people in the wineskins of our own culture and require buildings, budgets, educated and high-salaried clergy, and organizational models, all of which are foreign to them, and which they can't afford. And we wonder why our work among the poor is so pitiful, or why these poor people are such poor Presbyterians. This is inflexibility.

While we have been trying that approach and failing dismally, a Christian auto mechanic moves into a poor neighborhood and begins to earn his own way. He and his wife open their home on Sunday and invite acquaintances in to study the Bible and to sing. In the warmth and love of that home a church is born. As persons in the group have crises and needs, the little church shares its meager wealth to help out a friend and to do the works of mercy that characterize a Christian community. Within a year they have gotten so numerous that they don't fit in the livingroom anymore, but for a few dollars they are able to rent a large meeting room in the neighborhood. The gospel takes root. The church prospers, because without even knowing it this group has been adapted to the social, economic, and cultural milieu of these people.

At the other end of the economic spectrum is the well-known story of the late Sam Shoemaker of Pittsburgh. Dr. Shoemaker was the pastor of a large and wealthy Episcopal church. Many of the non-Christian friends of his parishioners would never darken the door of a church. So Sam Shoemaker took his Bible study evangelism into the country club, meeting them on their own turf, and the cause of the gospel flourished. That's imagination and innovation and flexibility.

I have on the wall of my study a poster, which says:

**But
we've always
done it
this
way!**

Brothers and sisters, the Spirit of God is the Creator Spirit. He is not locked into any one way of working. He is given to the church to equip it in each new day and in each new setting to herald the joyous news of the kingdom of God. He will give the Christian community grace to be available to special needs. He will inspire new forms and new expressions of music and worship. He will assist you to see the word of God afresh, and to discern the times. He will give understanding and boldness in the risky and radical confrontation with the systems of evil. He will lead you into merciful and costly ministries of the joyous news to the hapless victims of those systems. In the most demanding of circumstances he will equip you to be a source of praise unto God, who has called you to be his new humanity in Christ.

EPILOGUE
And Then the End Will Come

This has been only an introduction to the work of communicating the joyous news of the kingdom of God, the glad
tidings of Jesus Christ, to this present age. I have been deliberately kicking open doors and inviting you to look in, only to
hurry on to other dimensions of the work. I hope, thereby, to
provoke you to become excited with me over the work to which
our dear Lord has called us. What an enormous privilege it is,
and how utterly fulfilling!

Beyond the immediate joy of the work, though, is the one
clue to what determines the end of the age, when Jesus shall
return and the kingdom shall be consummated in all the thrill
and glory of that great day of the Lord. That determining factor
is this:

> "And this gospel of the kingdom will be preached
> throughout the whole world, as a testimony to all nations;
> and then the end will come."
>
> (Matt. 24:14)

Such a promise should motivate us to new zeal, more fervent
prayer, fresh hope, and boundless joy in the work of making
that gospel known. And to God be all praise!

The Lord be with you.

124706

NOTES

1. *Evangelism Manifesto* of the Christian Reformed Church and Reformed Churches in America, 1975.

2. Ibid.

3. Quoted in William Barclay, *The Letters to the Galatians and Ephesians* (Philadelphia: Westminster Press, 1958), p. 146.

4. *Book of Common Prayer,* Protestant Episcopal Church in the U.S.A., 1952, pp. 277–281.

5. J. D. Douglas, ed., *Let the Earth Hear His Voice* (Minneapolis, Minn.: World Wide Publications, 1975), p. 177.

6. Quoted in *The Post-American,* vol. 1, no. 1 (Fall 1971), p. 1.

7. Norval Geldenhuys, *Commentary on the Gospel of Luke* (Grand Rapids: William B. Eerdmans, 1952), p. 320.

8. From *Thoughts for Everyday Living,* by Maltbie D. Babcock (New York: Charles Scribner's Sons, 1901).

9. Stuart Briscoe, *Where Was the Church When the Youth Exploded?* (Grand Rapids: Zondervan, 1979).

JE